# Neurotic Money

## The World of Debt and How It Has Hijacked Your Brain

JOE ORNATO

Published by:

FriesenPress

Suite 300 – 852 Fort Street
Victoria, BC, Canada V8W 1H8

www.friesenpress.com

Distributed to the trade by The Ingram Book Company

# Table of Contents

*My 11-year-old son's impression of Neurotic Money*

*To my wife Maggie and my children Julia and Matteo:*
*You make me believe that what we imagine can come to life!*

# INTRODUCTION

Believe it or not, I read my first book, from start to finish, in 2005, at the age of thirty. I could get by in school by reading the bare minimum and using my ability to improvise in order to put concepts together and achieve results. I guess you could say that I was a smart kid but always used my ability to string together those concepts with a bit of "guessing" to make things work.

Anyway, my wife Maggie introduced me to the power of reading by making our family eliminate television for Lent that year. My first book was by Robin Sharma, a leadership book called *The Greatness Guide*. I devoured the content, which fuelled my passion for life. I have read an average of one book every two months since then, encompassing topics from leadership, business, economics, philosophy, psychology, history, spirituality and even neuro-science. Although most have been non-fiction, I have enjoyed the entertainment and education that come from books written by the likes of Paulo Coelho, Dan Brown and Ayn Rand, while TV is still a very limited part of our lives!

Books have taught me humility, patience, love and open-mindedness, but they have also illuminated my inner qualities of passion, strength and confidence. Books have inspired me to teach.

*Neurotic Money* is just that – a book that is intended to teach the reader all that I have learned about the mysterious world of money and debt. I can't sit here and write that I have all of the answers to your financial challenges, but I do have an answer – my answer! My answer includes over fifteen years of experience working with money, which includes banking, mortgage brokering, consulting, coaching and borrowing. Using all of these personal roles with respect to my relationship with money, I am able to thread connections to debt that most might not see, or choose not to see.

I have changed in the last fifteen years. I sold a very successful mortgage brokerage business in order to embrace a more simple life. My family lives on a 1-acre farm where we grow our own food, bake our own bread and raise our own chickens and rabbits. I gave up a six-figure income, and the debt that came with it, to unlearn everything that I thought I knew about money and debt. In the simplicity of my life, I was able to sort through the mental clutter of a typical North American lifestyle. As the song goes, *"I can see clearly now the rain is gone."*

The next chapter in my life has taught me what I didn't have time to learn while sitting behind a desk, negotiating with banks, working with customers and motivating staff to take our business to a new level. What I want you to learn from this book is that life changes, regardless of how bad things may look at any given time. Life will also throw you both good and bad experiences; however, all experiences are crucial for your own personal growth, *should you choose to learn from them.* Personal change begins with a choice. Consequently, financial change begins with a choice too. Sure, our choices take time to come to fruition, but when you make a choice, you set in motion a series of circumstances that will bring about what you desire. It'll happen – trust your life as it unfolds.

The feeling of being in debt or not fully understanding money is one of the biggest causes of stress in most people's lives. I have witnessed marriages fall apart because of money. Partnerships dissolve over money. Even governments perish because of money. However, money is really just a game. You need to learn aspects of the game just like a chess player learns how to play chess. The chess player will first learn basics, and then build on those basics by making mistakes in subsequent games. As each game comes and goes, the chess player gets a bit better. You too will get better at managing your debt. It's just a game – try to understand what the game makers are doing, and you'll notice that there is a way to win. This book will teach you that winning is becoming debt-free and having enough money to do what YOU desire, while being authentic to your dreams.

# MAGIC MONEY!

## WHAT IS MONEY?

Buying a LEGO™ set shouldn't be a complicated procedure, but that's what it turned into the day my son convinced me to take him to the toy store. Buying LEGO® is way more complicated than you think, especially when your son asks you, **"What is money, and why is it so important?"**

    *Dad: "Well, son, money gets us stuff."*
    *Son: "But other things get us stuff too, like when you give eggs to the neighbour and he lets us use his pool."*

    *Dad: "Money is worth something. It allows us to buy this LEGO®."*
    *Son: "Why only does money have value? It's only paper! I'd rather have LEGO®."*

    *Dad: "You're right, son, it's just paper."*
    *Son: "I have lots of paper at home."*

Hmmm…

*What is money?*

The truth is that the money we know and use today is simply made up of paper or metal. My conversation with my son perplexed me so much because I could not easily define money to him. Interestingly, I dug out my old economics textbook from university to help me clarify money's definition for myself. In the textbook *Economics In a Canadian Setting – Fellows, Flanagan, Shed & Waud,* money is defined as:

**"Money is any substance that performs the three functions of money. In short, money is what money does."**

Money *is* what money *does?*

I couldn't believe what I was reading! Who's saying this…Forrest Gump?

The game of money is so mysterious and magical that it can't really even be defined. In fact, the only definition it has in an economics course is what money can do, not what it really is.

Money performs three things:

1. Functions as a way to exchange goods and services;
2. Acts as a unit of value in order to measure things;
3. It stores value.

Money has value only by the fact that we, as humans, have faith that it will always perform the above-mentioned functions. Not only do we have faith in paper or coin, but we **trust** that our government will **guarantee** that our money is worth something, through thick and thin!

Money is something like playing a game of Monopoly™. As the game progresses, the winners will have accumulated more money than their opponents. During the game the **fake** money becomes so important to winning the game, that the players momentarily treat the Monopoly™ money as if it were real money!

You see, during the game, the players have faith that the Monopoly™ money *has true value* for the purpose of winning the game. The players never question whether the currency is real or not because it buys and sells property, collects rent and pays taxes.

Ironically, our **real** currency operates the same way. We, as consumers, investors, business owners, etc. have blind faith that our currency is worth what we are told by our governments. In our world, we place faith in government-fabricated paper and follow the rules set out by the banking system.

If you think comparing Monopoly™ money to real money is impossible, tell that to the Germans. By 1921, the German Deutschmark became so worthless because of hyperinflation that the German people used cigarettes and cognac as money! The point I am making is that ANYTHING can be money according to its definition, which makes the entire money system susceptible to change, manipulation and orchestration!

*A Simple History : The tale of the farmer, the wholesaler, the goldsmith and the creation of money*

The Farmer

I grew up with an Italian father who embraced the old school practice of farming on your land. Please don't misunderstand; we lived in the suburbs on less than an acre of land, but my father had the ability to make use of what he had.

When I did more research into my father's Italian roots, I discovered that Calabria (the province where my father was born) was among the poorest areas of Italy. You could either starve or work with what you had to survive. Luckily, my father had the work ethic to survive and instilled this in me. What intrigued me the most about my father's roots was the ability of the Calabrese people to barter. It was not uncommon for the Calabrese (people of Calabria) to trade eggs for sugar and flour for meat. In fact, my grandmother even breastfed for mothers who couldn't produce for their own children in return for goods that were needed by her family.

This is otherwise known as *barter* – I give you something that you need in exchange for something that I need. Goods and services are traded and there is no need for paper money as we know it today.

The major problem with the barter system is that when I don't need what you are offering in exchange for what I have, we can't make a deal that is fair for both of us. Let's assume that you are offering fruit for my crop of wheat. If I don't need your fruit, we don't have a deal. If the situation is reversed, and you don't need what I have, we still don't have a deal. However, what if I need your fruit but not until next Spring? We still have no deal unless we agree to exchange the wheat today for your fruit next Spring. Many traders and farmers engaged in barter exactly this way (I'll give you my wheat now in exchange for fruit next year), which is called *commodity money.*

The problem with commodity money is that if I give you my healthy wheat crop today, what happens if your fruit is damaged by floods next Spring? I have assumed all of the risk and have received no reward, yet you enjoyed my wheat crop today. The other issue is that the value of what we are trading is subject to what we think they're worth at the time of our need. There is no universal acceptance of a unit of value.

The Wholesaler

It was now time for the wholesaler to solve the problems of commodity money.

Toward the end of the Middle Ages, Italian wholesale traders in textiles, clothing, wine, metals and all sorts of other commodities had to trust their purchasers for the products that they had supplied them. They used the trustworthiness of the purchaser to issue a *bill of exchange* and a promise to pay for the goods when they received the money from the eventual sale.

The bills of exchange were then used as forms of payment based on the credit worthiness of the purchaser, and thus, another form of money was created. England used these bills of exchange well into the 18th century, before banknotes (www.en.wikipedia.org/wiki/history_of_money).

If we trace the origins of money back a bit further, Pheidon, King of Argos, Greece is attributed to creating the first known coins in the 7th century BC. Many countries and civilizations created their own coin from all types of metal, which proved to be inefficient. What was valued in one country was not necessarily accepted in another. Moreover, various metals could be manipulated, forged or even clipped and recycled into other materials.

The Goldsmith

At the same time that bills of exchange were being used to transact and trade, gold, too, was one of the most popular mediums of exchange used to purchase goods and services. Those who had gold wanted to protect it, so the goldsmith offered to store people's gold in his vault for a fee, much like how we keep money in a bank account or a safety deposit box today.

After a while, the goldsmith built a good reputation for keeping people's gold safe but realized that only a few of his clients would actually come and demand to take out their gold at any one time. Rather than lugging around several hundred ounces of gold in their pockets, the goldsmith offered his customers slips of paper indicating the value of gold they had stored in his vault. Customers, knowing that they could retrieve their gold at anytime, would make up IOU slips and trade them with each other on the premise that they could redeem one's IOU for another's gold, should they need to. What began happening is that the IOUs became just as valuable as the gold. The IOUs, or paper, quickly replaced the gold people used to purchase things. However, everyone knew (or so they thought) that they could redeem those IOUs for their gold anytime they wanted.

Suddenly, the goldsmith had an idea. What if he could create his own IOU slips based on the inventory of gold he stored for others, lend them out to others as loans and charge interest on those loans? In essence, he began making money on other people's money. He knew that only a few of his customers would come and claim their gold at any one time, so even when his depositors demanded to see their gold (they suspected that the goldsmith was cheating them), the goldsmith would open the vault and show that the gold was safe.

It should be noted that the lending out of gold that did not belong to them was not ethical or even legal, but the human trait of greed superseded honesty and integrity! - *Economics in a Canadian Setting, p. 731, footnote 3*

Once the gold depositors figured out what the goldsmith was doing and how much money he was making, they demanded to get in on the scheme. Customers began investing more gold with the goldsmith and the cycle continued of lending out IOUs for people to perform the three functions of money. The interest earned on loans would be pure profit for the gold smith and his depositors, but he always ensured that his depositors received less on the deposits while he received more on the loans. The goldsmith's IOU practice and the wholesaler's bill of exchange practice were the foundations for the creation of the "paper" money we know and value today.

*Faith-based money* was created. I call it "faith-based" money because the depositor had to have faith that the goldsmith was keeping his gold safe and could access it at anytime, all based on a paper slip. However, I may be drawing an inaccurate conclusion, because in reality, all of the goldsmith's customers could, in fact, redeem their IOUs for gold whenever they wanted to, right? In other words, the paper IOUs were *guaranteed* by gold reserves held by the goldsmith. As far as the depositor was concerned, gold was the standard of measuring the value of money, and if the depositor had $100 in IOUs, that meant he had $100 worth of gold on deposit with the goldsmith.

In reality, though, the goldsmith based his system of redemption on statistical evidence and chance. The goldsmith's success depended on the principle that not everyone needed their money at the same time, so he would lend out more IOUs than he had gold on deposit.

*****

### Modern Day Money, Fractional Reserve Banking and the Abolition of Gold as a Standard of Measurement

The modern day banking system operated the same, just like the goldsmith, until the 1920s and 1930s. Each dollar was redeemable for gold. The United States created the Federal Reserve Bank, which is essentially the banker to the bankers. The irony was that there really wasn't as much gold as there was paper, so if an investor such as a foreign country wanted to redeem their dollars for gold, the money tree could break.

During World War I, many central bankers feared that if major countries holding dollars would demand that they exchange their dollars for gold, the banking system would collapse because they wouldn't have enough gold. This is commonly referred to as a "run on the bank." Our bankers were doing exactly what the goldsmith taught us – lending out IOU slips as money and hoping like hell that only a few of their customers would actually want their gold at the same time!

Consequently, even if the banks' customers were not smart enough to figure out that the paper money they were given by their bank was based on gold that potentially didn't exist, the big players in government and big business sure did! A run on the bank is when too many customers ask to have their money back in their hands, be it gold or paper money. If the bank is lending out currency based on its customers not cashing their money out, it can be forced to shut down when an unusually high percentage of its customers demand to have their money in a short period of time. Many banks have been shut down, contributing to catastrophic losses for their customers and investors. In fact, the stock market crash in 1929 was, in part, influenced by "runs on the banks."

In response to this threat, many central banks and governments rid themselves of the gold standard, effectively detaching their currency from gold. Now dollars were "legal tender," which meant that one dollar was worth another dollar because the government says so! Declaration-based money, or *fiat money*, was created. Now central banks and governments could create as much money as they wanted because they did not have to worry about holding gold reserves in exchange for money.

Removing the gold standard from our money doesn't mean that banks are immune from a "run." In fact, if all of a bank's customers demanded that their money be withdrawn from their bank accounts in a short period of time, the same collapse would occur. The difference (without gold as a standard) is that now our money supply can be manipulated by regulators and central bankers so that new money can be printed and supplied to the bank in trouble. Still better for the bankers, the troubled banks could be bought at a discount! Recently, the banks of Iceland suffered because of "runs," were bailed out and are now essentially owned by policy makers!

Let's take a look at a recent list of Wikipedia's "runs on banks."

*Recent "runs on banks" according to Wikipedia, 26 November 2009*

*1990s*
*\* In 1999, a bank run happened in Malaysia where Bank Negara Malaysia (the Malaysian central bank) had to take control of MBf Finance Berhad, the biggest finance company in Malaysia during that time. Many of the finance company's 120 branches saw runs on their deposits, totaling about 17 billion Ringgit (US$4.49 billion).[2]*

*2000s*
*\* In 2001, during the Argentine economic crisis (1999-2002), a bank run and corralito was experienced in Argentina. There are various theories into the cause.[3] This contributed towards the bank runs in neighbouring Uruguay during the 2002 Uruguay banking crisis.*

*\* In early August 2007, Countrywide Financial, an American firm, suffered a bank run as a consequence of the subprime mortgage crisis.[4]*

*\* On 13 September 2007, the British bank Northern Rock arranged an emergency loan facility from the Bank of England, which it claimed was the result of short-term liquidity problems. The resulting bank run*

was not the traditional form, where depositors withdraw money in a snowball effect, leading to a liquidity crisis; instead, it occurred after news reports of a liquidity crisis that was not a bank run.[5] The resulting financial crisis ended with the nationalisation of Northern Rock.[6]

* On Tuesday, 11 March 2008, a bank run began on the securities and banking firm Bear Stearns. While Bear Stearns was not an ordinary deposit-taking bank, it had financed huge long-term investments by selling short-maturity bonds (Asset-Backed Commercial Paper), making it vulnerable to panic on the part of its bondholders. Credit officers of rival firms began to say that Bear Stearns would not be able to make good on its obligations. Within two days, Bear Stearns' capital base of $17 billion had dwindled to $2 billion in cash, and Bear Stearns told government officials that it saw little option other than to file for bankruptcy the next day. By 07:00 Friday, the Federal Reserve decided to lend Bear Stearns money, the first time it had lent to a nonbank since the Great Depression. Stocks sank, and that day, JP Morgan Chase began an effort to buy Bear Stearns as part of a government-sponsored bailout. The deal was arranged by Sunday in an effort to calm markets before overseas markets opened.[7]

* On 11 July 2008, U.S. mortgage lender IndyMac Bank was seized by federal regulators. the bank relied heavily on higher cost, less stable, brokered deposits, as well as secured borrowings, to fund its operations and focused on stated income and other aggressively underwritten loans in areas with rapidly escalating home prices, particularly in California and Florida.[8] A highly stressed institution,[9] IndyMac's capital was being lost to downgrades as the poor quality of their books was revealed.[10] Regulators at the Office of Thrift Supervision (OTS) had allowed the bank to misstate its financial condition, avoiding regulatory intervention.[11][12] On 26 June, Sen. Charles E. Schumer released to the media some letters he had sent to regulators, which warned that the bank might not be viable. In the days following the release, depositors pulled out approximately 7.5% of the bank's deposits.[13][14] IndyMac

*and the OTS regulators who had allowed the bank to backdate its books blamed Schumer's letters for the bank's demise. These regulators resigned or were fired amidst a Treasury Department investigation.[15][16][17] IndyMac's failure is expected to have cost the FDIC about $9 billion. [18] Uninsured depositors have lost an estimated $270 million.[19]*

*\* On 25 September 2008, the Office of Thrift Supervision was forced to shut down Washington Mutual, the largest savings and loan in the United States and the sixth-largest overall financial institution, due to a massive run. Over the previous 10 days, customers had withdrawn $16.7 billion in deposits. This is currently the biggest bank failure in American financial history. Normally, banks are seized on Fridays to allow the FDIC the weekend to prepare the failed bank for takeover by another bank. However, WaMu's size led regulators to shut it down on a Thursday.[20][21][22]*

*\* On 6 October 2008, Landsbanki, Iceland's second largest bank, was put into government receivership. The Icelandic government used emergency powers to dismiss the board of directors of Landsbanki and took control of the failed institution. Prime Minister Geir Haarde also rushed measures through parliament to give the country's largest bank, Kaupthing, a £400m loan. In addition, Iceland pleaded with Russia to extend 3bn in credit, as western countries refused to help.[23] With over 5bn in savings held by Britons in Landsbanki, the Icelandic collapse threatened private citizens in the United Kingdom as well as companies in Iceland.[24]*

This practice of bailing out banks has even extended to corporations such as General Motors and Chrysler! This goes to show just how money can be manipulated and that it can serve just about anyone's agenda with complete disregard for the wellbeing of its citizens!

## The Fractional Reserve System: Truly fractured!

Simply put, a fractional reserve banking system requires banks to keep on deposit a certain ratio of real paper money to accommodate for withdrawals of cash, just like the goldsmith kept a percentage of gold on hand in case of redemption, known as a "fractional reserve." The banks needed to keep a "fraction" of the money on deposit in case of redemption. The most common fractional reserve ratio that the banks used was 10%, so for every $10 a bank had in deposits, they could lend out $9 90% in credit.

Here's a different way of looking at the same numbers: Let's assume that your parents deposit $10,000 into their savings account. Their bank would be allowed to lend out $9,000 in the form a loan to you. You take that $9,000 loan and pay a vendor for a car, and that vendor deposits it into his/her bank account at another bank. That bank now has $9,000 on deposit so it can now lend out $8,100 in credit, and the cycle continues. The result is that our banks create money out of credit. In this case, we have created $27,100 ($10,000 + $9000 +8100) in new money from the initial $10,000 deposit, yet the amount of real money in the system was really only $10,000! As long as the 10% reserve was accounted for, our banks could lend 90% of the deposit to another, even if the original deposit came from money borrowed. Essentially, one's debt becomes another's deposit!

The fractional reserve system is designed to keep <u>some</u> of their customers' money at the bank, but if (think about this practically) we all asked for our bank account savings in cash, the banks could collapse. In reality, most of the money that banks account for as an asset, was, at one time or another, borrowed from somewhere else! I recently read a statistic that stated that if all the cash in our monetary system were cashed in for paper money and coin, you'd end up with approximately only 3% of the money in the system; the rest is created by credit! No wonder we are being bombarded by new credit card offers everyday!

## Getting Rid of Reserves

You would think that keeping at least 10% of their customers' money on hand is a prudent practice and that it is already a risky procedure, but as the banking system grew, so did its risk of having too many customers want their money at the same time. Once again, our central bankers stepped in and changed the reserve requirements. Since The Bank Act was revised in 1992, Canadian Banks actually don't have to keep any reserves at all:

*457.*

*(4) On the first day of the first month following the month this section comes into force, the primary reserve referred to in subsection (2) shall be reduced by 3 per cent, and thereafter on the first day of the first month of each of the next three succeeding six month periods, the primary reserve as modified by this subsection shall be reduced by 3 per cent, and on the first day of the twenty-fifth month following the month in which this section comes into force, the primary reserve referred to in subsection (1) shall be nil.*

## What does this mean for consumers?

This is the million dollar question! What this means to me is that our dependency on credit helps our banks create a false sense of value. Our banks' profits are dependant on credit being expanded through borrowers such as you and I. That expansion of the money supply is leveraged even more when corporations try to lend each other money. Still bigger, governments try to borrow so they can finance public works projects and try to make their countries better for their citizens, or so they say.

We are a microcosm of the bigger picture. Money is expanding everywhere, but it really is only debt that someone else deposited. As quickly as the money system can grow with the extension of debt and NO banking reserves, it can come crashing down. The United States is an example of the havoc a credit squeeze can have on an economy. Several European countries have gone bankrupt! *When the debt ain't flowing, money ain't growing!*

The point I am trying to make here is that if we rely on debt to buy more now, we expose ourselves to great financial risk when our monetary system expands and contracts! If money is created out of new debt that is deposited at another bank and then is lent out with zero reserve fund requirements, what happens when money starts to shrink? What happens when central bankers decide to whom and for what price will they lend? What happens when banks cannot lend as much because borrowers are losing jobs? What happens when those who have money start to save and refuse to borrow or spend? What happens when bank profits start to dwindle because they can't lend, and no one wants to borrow? What happens when governments can't pay their debts on time?

*We are, in retrospect, slaves to our banks. The amount of credit we each have dictates just how heavy our balls and chains are!*

The topic of debt is a hot topic in the news. We are told we are in a recession, so our government is justified in running a deficit, meaning that the government is spending more than it is bringing in. This adds to the national debt. Where did this money come from? Who lent it? How will it be paid back? What if an entire nation stopped believing that their money was worth anything?

Money is essentially magic! Like the alchemist who transforms metal to gold, our governments and bankers turn paper into value.

Money does irrational things to itself and to people. It can help and it can hinder, but mystic and magical … it will always be.

> *"You're right, son, it's just paper."*
> *"I have lots of paper at home …"*

… So do the bankers. Except now, with the advent of technology, they don't even need paper anymore, just an abundance of digits!

## Quotes for Thought:

*"The modern banking system manufactures money out of nothing. The process is perhaps the most astounding piece of sleight of hand that was ever invented. Banking was conceived in inequity and born in sin … Bankers own the earth. Take it away from them but leave them the power to create money, and, with a flick of a pen, they will create enough money to buy it back again. … Take this great power away from them and all great fortunes like mine will disappear, for then this would be a better and happier world to live in. … But, if you want to continue to be the slaves of bankers and pay the cost of your own slavery, then let bankers continue to create money and control credit." – Sir Josiah Stamp, president of the Bank of England and the second richest man in Britain in the 1920s.*

*"We are completely dependent on the commercial Banks. Someone has to borrow every dollar we have in circulation, cash or credit. If the Banks create ample synthetic money we are prosperous; if not, we starve. We are absolutely without a permanent money system. When one gets a complete grasp of the picture, the tragic absurdity of our hopeless position is almost incredible, but there it is. It is the most important subject intelligent persons can investigate and reflect upon." – Robert H. Hemphill, Credit Manager of the Federal Reserve Bank of Atlanta in the Great Depression, 1934*

*"Banks create money. That is what they are for. ... The manufacturing process to make money consists of making an entry in a book. That is all. ... Each and every time a Bank makes a loan ... new Bank credit is created — brand new money."* – Graham Towers, Governor of the Bank of Canada from 1935 to 1955

*"When a bank makes a loan, it simply adds to the borrower's deposit account in the bank by the amount of the loan. The money is not taken from anyone else's deposit; it was not previously paid in to the bank by anyone. It's new money, created by the bank for the use of the borrower."* – Robert B. Anderson, Secretary of the Treasury under Eisenhower, said in an interview reported in the August 31, 1959 issue of U.S. News and World Report

*"Whenever destroyers appear among men, they start by destroying money, for money is men's protection and the base of moral existence. Destroyers seize gold and leave to its owners a counterfeit pile of paper. This kills all objective standards and delivers men into the arbitrary power of an arbitrary setter of values. Gold was the objective value, and equivalent of wealth produced. Paper is a mortgage on wealth that does not exist, backed by a gun aimed at those who are expected to produce it. Paper is a check drawn by legal looters upon an account which is not theirs: upon the virtue of victims. Watch for the day when it bounces, marked: Account overdrawn."* Ayn Rand, Atlas Shrugged copyright 1957

## Questions for Self-Reflection:

1. **What did you learn about the creation of money from this chapter?**
2. **What do the practices of the goldsmith and the U.S. mortgage meltdown in 2007 have in common?**
3. **Is a financial meltdown of our money system possible in theory?**

# MONEY
# ALWAYS CHANGES!

Although we have retraced the steps of how money came to be, it should be noted that money will always continue to change and redefine itself! Don't believe me?

Between 2007 and 2008, some of the world's largest financial institutions collapsed. When you look at the financial disaster that occurred in 2008, with governments having to bail out banks, insurance companies and auto makers, it is obvious that the concept of money has changed. You see, the financial disaster was orchestrated by a combination of too much consumer debt (money borrowed), an inflated housing bubble (money as an asset), and the use of derivatives (money created on the concept that money would be created sometime in the future: in other words, speculation). Money can be created, manipulated and changed. In fact, there are many more types of money today than ever before, and you might not have even noticed them.

Reward points such as Airmiles® are really a form of money. You can earn them and exchange them for a good or service of value. Remember? *Money is what money does.* Even the local pet store has created a new form of money; for every purchase, you get a stamp, and then at the tenth stamp, the next purchase is free. Canadian

Tire Corporation has been using their own form of money for decades! New forms of money are being created everyday, but the change that will impact us the most in the future is the creation of *digital money*.

It surprised me when I last renewed my passport. I obtained the form, filled in the applicable information, took my pictures, obtained my guarantors and proceeded to the local passport office. When it came time to pay for my renewal fee, I had noticed a sign that indicated only debit, cheque or credit card were accepted. Our very own government was refusing to accept cash – the same cash that it declares as legal tender!

The more society embraces a culture in which cash is out but automation and digital money are in, I fear that indebtedness will continue to rise until more financial disasters strike, both at the personal and national levels. Only then will the concept of money be transformed into a medium of exchange that commands self-discipline and strategy.

Digital money and automation also take advantage of flaws in the human brain. As you will see in the next section, big business, banks and governments just happen to have research on their side. Unless the consumer becomes educated in just how you make decisions (biologically and culturally), you'll never be able to battle the product arsenal that corporations and banks sell you in order to maximize their profits at your expense.

**Questions for reflection:**

1. **How many different reward programs do you have?**
2. **How can you better use these reward programs to get out of debt and increase cashflow?**

# I'M NOT SICK - I JUST HAVE A SMALL ACHE

Have you ever noticed that when someone is diagnosed with a disease such as cancer, it is usually right after they complain about a minor ache or ailment? In some instances, there isn't even an ache, but the diagnosis happens after a routine check-up!

The minor ache continues until that person decides to finally go and have it checked out, only to be sent for further testing and then finally being given the grim news about a terminal illness.

Most people tell me that they wish they could lead healthier lives – that they wish they had the time to eat right, exercise daily and schedule routine check-ups. Why do we do this only after disaster strikes? What is most tragic is that we know we need to make changes to see different results in our lives, yet we allow ourselves to deteriorate despite our knowledge.

Then there are those who might not have the knowledge and fail to ask questions to gain the knowledge they need to achieve what they want in life. If we just took some time to look at our symptoms or ask the right questions, we could prevent the causes to our pain and suffering.

We all have symptoms of some sort when it comes to our finances too! Just as the patient who goes in for a headache and finds out she has cancer, the borrower seeks to refinance his mortgage to consolidate debt. As seen commonly in mainstream medicine, most financial experts will simply prescribe another "pill" to cover up the root causes of financial chaos and inefficiency.

When you don't treat the causes of debt and cash mismanagement, bankruptcy is the ultimate result, or you become stuck in what Robert Kiyosaki, author of "Rich Dad Poor Dad," calls "The Rat Race." You'll work your life away in order to pay for that bigger home, that fancier car, those competitive children's sports and that take-out food, all while struggling to save money for retirement. The kicker is that these items are often financed, not spent based on cash-flow planning. Retirement creeps up on you quicker than you think, but the stark reality for so many Canadians is old age, no retirement, no money and more work than they ever had!

This concept is hard for most people to swallow because we have been trained by major banks that debt is a simple and acceptable process; the banks train us to borrow for things we can't afford with cash and make payments until the debt is paid back. The debt is amortized or stretched out so that banks profit from our lack of focus, clarity and bad habits. Banks set up a trap that shifts our focus from our long term goals and the consequences of our choices today to what interest rate we get and what prepayment options are available. They neglect to tell us that if we changed certain habits and set up disciplined spending structures, we could be debt-free faster; they distract us by telling us to pay bi-weekly or monthly; they play games with our money by negotiating the interest rate on your debt and then saying, "go shop around to find a better deal, and we'll match it." We have become so disoriented by the features and benefits of debt products that we ignore the impact of this debt on our lives and don't plan how we're going to pay it off!

When it comes to choice, we, as consumers, have never had so many! It's not coincidental that the market is flooded with product choices. There is so much choice being offered in disguise as having your best interests at heart, but the reality is this: *give them so much choice that, through all of the confusion, they'll miss the big picture, spend more and stay in debt for longer than if they could think strategically.*

*Think ... strategically ... hmmm ...*

Could it be that there is another major contributor to the unprecedented levels of debt in North America? I mean, here I am, blaming the banks for their system of entrapment, but aren't we all grown-ups here? Did we get ourselves into this mess in the first place? How?

Our brains have a lot to do with how we spend money. I have even heard of the term "neuro-economics," which explains the relationship between the functions of our brains and money!

In this next section, we'll devote ourselves to understanding just how our culture, attitudes and certain parts of our brain contribute to our excessive spending and debt levels. We'll understand just how we contributed to our levels of spending and debt just as much as the bankers have. It's not all bad news though! As much as the brain can be manipulated to line the pockets of banks and big business, it can be molded and trained to help you build the financial future you want to see.

*"The richest man in the world, I've since discovered, isn't the person who has the most, but the one who needs the least."*
*Robin Sharma-The Saint, The Surfer & The CEO*

## Questions for Self-Analysis

1. What financial habits do I have that I know I should change but haven't because I'm procrastinating?
2. What were my last three purchases, and did I pay for them with cash instead of credit?
3. What could I be doing to pay off my debt quicker?

# ATTITUDES, CULTURE
# AND EVOLUTION

**Attitude Swimmers, Surfers, Drowners and Sailors, Which one are you?**

The Wizard Academy is a 21st Century Business School in Texas. I first came across this ultra-unique style of continuing education by subscribing to *The Monday Morning Memo*, a weekly blog that Roy H. Williams, the founder, sends to his email list of recipients.

I was enrolled in the website and blog creation course, but one of the perks was an opportunity to meet Roy H. Williams in person and listen to some of his wisdom. He told us a story about swimmers, surfers, drowners and sailors, which conveyed a message simply about our attitudes in life.

He said swimmers are those who seem to ride the currents of the ocean and get pushed around and end up wherever they end up and don't really think otherwise about it.

Surfers, on the other hand, get excited every time a new wave (known as a gimmick) comes along, and then they ride those waves, chasing a new one wherever it shows up. This also means that Surfers end up wherever because they ride each gimmick in any direction without a clear destination, not realizing that all waves are part of the ocean.

Drowners are those who professionally see the world through foggy goggles, where the world acts upon them, and they see their circumstances as the primary cause of pain in life. Drowners see only doom and gloom and are on a mission to take everyone to the bottom of the ocean with them.

Sailors are those who pick their destination, lock their destination and adjust their course to the currents and waves as needed in order to achieve their goal.

It is ironic that in finances, too, we tend to fall into one of these four categories.

Some of us accept our debt and spending habits "as is" and really don't care about much except that there is enough to live in the moment. We spend on autopilot and wonder in amazement why we have so much debt while swimming and paddling to make the payments and stay afloat.

Then there those of us who are always looking for the next product or best deal (wave) and get extremely excited about how that specific product is going to change our circumstances only to find out that the wave eventually disappears. We pick up our surf boards and wait for the next wave, allowing the wave to take us anywhere. Although riding the wave is thrilling, it will come and go and is not useful in traveling long distances.

Drowners are those who blame the stock market or the bank or their spouse for financial challenges. I find that there are more of us who act this way than we'd like to admit. Drowners jump into the ocean of debt and fail to swim, surf or sail. They just complain about their circumstances, yet they made the decision to jump into the ocean in the first place. Need I say more??? I am depressed just writing about this group!

Finally, Sailors don't wait, ride the trend or blame. Rather, they lock their sight on what their life goals are and what it is that their finances are supposed to achieve in relation to those goals. First of all, they use a boat filled with knowledge that will keep them afloat while they use financial products to help them navigate the ocean to their destination. Sailors often recruit professionals to help on board and make their journey easier. Of course, there will be challenges, waves, currents and even some storms, but the sailor is able to sustain the course because of using the right boat, the right equipment and the right crew.

Where do you want to go? How will you navigate the ocean in order to achieve your purpose? If you've never really thought about it, then how do you know where exactly you're going to go?

*In order to clarify our goals, we must first understand exactly why we spend the way we do. An attitude adjustment is a powerful way to start!*

*Whatever you can do or dream you can, begin it. Boldness has a genius and magic in it. Begin it now. Goeth*

**Questions for Reflection**

1. **Are you a Swimmer, Surfer, Drowner or Sailor?**
2. **Are there times when you have been a combination of each?**
3. **Who are the people in your life who exemplify sailors and how can you learn from them?**

**Attitude and Culture**

On Wednesday, 14 September 2011, The Royal Bank of Canada released a survey that read: **Canadians Comfortable With Debt.**

**Translation:** *Canadians Too Embarrassed To Admit That They Have Too Much Debt!*

An uncommon conversation that you would have heard at BBQs all over the country this past Summer would have been,

*"I have been horrible with my finances. I keep getting into more debt because I can't control my urges to buy more things. I seem to justify everything I purchase and use the excuse that interest rates are low, so it makes total sense to borrow instead of pay cash. However, I don't have cash, so borrowing is my only option, and I really did need the new car – it's way more efficient on gas than my old car."*

To my surprise, the survey said that 70% of Canadians are *comfortable* with their debt. Astonishingly, 75% *believed* that they were in *better shape* than their neighbor! (Meanwhile the debt-to-income ratio is at an all time high of 148%! This means that for every dollar of income you earn per year, you'll owe the equivalent of $1.48 in debt.

The reason the RBC survey projected the results it did, was because of a phenomenon psychologists call *The Framing Effect.* In essence, humans have the ability to re-frame or adjust the picture to fit the frame based on how information is presented *(p.148 PSYCH Rathus, Maheu, Veenlient).* In other words, we'll see what we believe we are presented and, in this case, we see that our debt is at a level that's "comfortable." Statistics Canada, on the other hand, shows that we have moved beyond comfort and into unchartered territory with respect to our debt and our income. Who in their right mind would believe that having debt worth 148% of their income is comfortable?

The irony of the RBC survey is that RBC is a bank. In fact, they are Canada's largest bank. Banks make money based on lending. If lending stops, so do huge profit margins. Moreover, if the financial turmoil that the United States has suffered were to spill over into Canada in the same way, the banks would be crippled.

In my opinion, the RBC survey reveals three things: First, it is designed to keep Canadians in the frame of mind that debt is an accepted way of life and borrowing is just part of the Canadian dream! Second, the survey is designed to encourage those Canadians who are struggling with debt to keep making those payments; besides, according to the survey, you are in better shape than your neighbour! Third, this survey shows just how our culture has come to accept excessive debt.

As a culture, we accept debt so much that our debts are not talked about in the open, like the example of the summer BBQ. Debt is just a way of getting by in a Canadian setting, and nobody questions it otherwise. Let's face it, debt is not comfortable, yet we portray in surveys that it is. Again, debt has become engrained in our livelihoods, and it shows in our habits, our purchases and our entertainment.

In this day of reality television, it never ceases to amaze me just how profoundly reality shows play out in the lives of everyday people. Moreover, reality television caters to what the culture of a nation wants to watch. It just so happens that other people's problems become our entertainment. On top of that, reality television attempts to exploit the very worst of a situation for ratings. Never will you see the average family who *can* afford their bills but just can't seem to get ahead be on the show *Till Debt Do Us Part*. It is the family with excessive spending habits, overdue credit cards, late mortgage payments, addictions and marital problems who get the stardom! Viewers are relieved that there are people in worse situations than their own.

The reality is that it is the *average* family who will dramatically suffer, should interest rates rise 2 or 3% over the next few years (oh yeah, you had better bank on that!). It is the *average* family who *can* afford their debts payments now but have little left over for anything else. It is these people who are in the worst situations, but the media seeks ratings, and ratings are high when the audience is made to feel superior to those they watch! When the *average* family fails to make their payments because of a spike in interest rates, the economic system feels the pain. The United States showed this in 2008. Canada has yet to experience this, but I can assure you that we're not far off!

It's time to come to the realization that we have become a culture of debt, and despite what your banks says, its time to change that cultural attitude and go through some short-term pain now in order to avert a financial crisis in your family later!

### Exercise to Combat Overconfidence

When we are faced with the realization that a past decision that we had made was wrong, our brains fumble around and look for a way of justifying what we knew all along. Once a decision has revealed its consequence, we use hindsight to explain our decisions.

Overconfidence is a symptom of being so convinced with your decision that you'll overlook other important factors in making that choice. Our debt is no different. As a former mortgage broker and banker, I listened to clients explain their decisions to get into debt and justify their purchases. Why do we become overconfident, even when the statistics show us that we're wrong? The text book *PSYCH, by Rathus Maheu and Veenvliet (p. 149)*, shows us that overconfidence is produced because:

- We tend to be unaware of how flimsy our judgments may be.
- We tend to focus on examples that confirm our judgments and ignore those that do not.
- Our working memories have limited space; we tend to forget information that runs counter to our judgments.
- We work to bring about the events we believe in, so sometimes they become self-fulfilling prophecies.

The good news is that the same process for becoming overconfident and then getting yourself into debt can be reversed. Just take the above process that got you into debt and work backward:

1. **Did I educate and research enough about this financial decision?**
2. **Should I ask friends and family for assistance on educating me? What is the worst case scenario in making this decision?**
3. **What are all the factors that impact this decision, both good and bad, and have I written them out?**
4. **What exactly do I want to see with my finances in the future? Did I write this out?**

# EVOLUTION

**Consumer Spending: Nature's Gift Gone Wrong?**

Did we, as human beings, evolve to spend?

When we study the history of life on Earth, it is inarguable that many things have changed over time. Even the whale as we know it today, had legs and roamed land before its legs evolved to eventually become non-existent:

> *In 1997, Gingerich and Uhen noted that whales "... have a fossil record that provides remarkably complete evidence of one of life's great evolutionary adaptive radiations: transformation of a land mammal ancestor into a diversity of descendant sea creatures."–source: http://www.agiweb.org/news/evolution/examplesofevolution.html*

When the peacock is seeking a partner, he will go through great lengths to ensure his feathers are well oiled, bright and big! The features on those feathers are considered *fitness indicators.*

Humans have changed over the millions of years, and it's evolution is the premise of **Geoffrey Miller's book, "Spent:** *sex, evolution and consumer behavior."*

Human tribes would use "fitness indicators" to gain social status and attract optimal mates. Just as the peacock oils his feathers, so too does Johnny wet down his hair when he sees a mirror! Fitness indicators are signals of a person's traits and qualities that are perceived by others. Unfortunately, fitness indicators are rarely conscious. Rather, they are subconscious, such as the size of a mane on a lion, the shape of a shark's fin or the stature of a gorilla – the features are there, and the opposite sex doesn't consciously realize why, but there is an attraction.

Humans have natural fitness indicators, such as strength, odor, and sexual drive, but we have evolved the abilities to create, imagine, demonstrate and play out new types of fitness indicators. This explains the difference between women falling all over Brad Pitt, while Johnny from down the road, although good-looking, doesn't stand a chance going up against a movie star such as Pitt! However, these newer fitness indicators are cultural and social, rather than biological. In essence, we have evolved so that we are attracted to traits such as popularity, fame and fortune instead of our primal indicators of strength, hunting and sexual reproductive abilities.

We are social primates who survive and reproduce largely through attracting practical support from kin, friends and mates. We only receive that support when others view us as having desirable traits that fulfill *their* needs, such as the woman who is attracted to an extremely strong man. Her attraction is for the sole benefit of her protection, whether she is conscious of this or not. In tribal times, strength meant much more than it does today because tribes were at war with each other, whereas today, we live in a rather peaceful country.

Over the past few million years, we have evolved many mental and moral ways of showing those desirable traits, one of which is the accumulation of wealth and social status.

Could it be that our historical fitness indicators of reproduction, strength and hunting ability have been masked or replaced by newer fitness indicators that unconsciously demonstrate the same primal ones?

Does owning a big home subconsciously represent hierarchy of power instead of tribal competitions, which, ultimately, means strength? Does having two cars signify self-protection instead of running away from danger? Does having the newest electronic devices make us more socially appealing than elongated nose rings did for tribes, signaling an ability to procreate?

Ultimately, we think that we purchase products and services based on what pleasure they'll give us. How others will perceive us when we have such things is often more important. According to Geoffrey Miller, consumerism is really a form of narcissism.

What is ironic about most of the things on which we tend to spend money is that the most luxurious items we buy are the least essential to human survival. I guarantee that the new big screen TV won't put any extra food on the table tonight!

It's time to get back to basics in terms of human existence. We have to take control of our finances and focus on what's important in *our* lives and forget what others will think of us! More importantly, we have to try to become conscious of why we spend the way we do.

A good start is to use the question *"Will this purchase truly change my life?"* It has worked for my family for years, and in 99% of the spending decisions with which I am faced, the answer is an overwhelming NO!

**Exercise for Self-Improvement**

**The Magic Question**

**On the next item that you are tempted to buy, whether it is groceries, coffee or clothes, ask yourself The Magic Question:**

**Will this purchase change my life?**

Try it on the next purchase and then write down *why* this purchase will change your life. Chances are that you'll start to see the ludicrousness in most of your purchases, and you'll begin to make smarter purchases.

# THE NAG FACTOR

One would think that considering your child to be a powerful influencer of what you buy would be dramatic and quite an overstatement, but the truth is that children influence approximately $600 billion USD in product sales each year. Children aged five to fourteen directly affect $196 billion, while indirectly affecting $400 billion annually. *(The Kids Market – March 2000).*

On top of that, corporations that target children as one of the most lucrative sources of revenue will have an impact in your spending habits as a family and, consequently, the amount of debt you owe! Corporations have hired psychologists and neurologists to exploit the vulnerability of your child so that you open your pocketbook. Essentially, corporations have embraced the motto that your child is a consumer from "cradle to grave" *(Consuming Kids – Susan Linn).*

It is also estimated that children are exposed to an average of 90 minutes of television each day by the time they are 6 months old. What's worse is that the marketers for the corporations know the infamous Jean Piaget's work (Piaget was a psychologist), where he discovered just how the development of children's intellect played out. However, the most important part of his work (for the marketers) was that children go through a stage of "sensory motor development." Infants learn through touch and taste but may learn even more through sound and vision. *(Consuming Kids – Susan Linn).*

With the use of excessive media, we are breeding a generation of children who first learn to identify with a *brand* rather than a personal relationship. Corporations know this, but we, as parents, miss the seduction until it's too late.

Another fascinating observation occurred to me when I came across a concept called *"The Nag Factor."* According to a study by Western Media International and Lieberman Research Worldwide, it is parents who are divorced and those with teens or small children who give in the most to nagging. More importantly, the study reveals to companies just how much nagging will influence a parent to purchase a product. More than one quarter of all the visits to theme parks were a direct result of nagging. *(The Corporation – a documentary by Joel Bakan).* Major corporations, including banks, are armed with more insight into your child's behavior, reactions and learning than you.

In the same documentary, Lucy Hughes of Western Media International (now Initiative Media Worldwide) justifies marketing to your child this way:

> *"If we understand what motivates a parent to buy a product … if we develop, you know, a thirty second commercial that encourages a child to whine … that the child understands and is able to reiterate to the parents, then we're successful."*

Conclusively, implanting the concept of consuming products and services at such a young age, we have inadvertently molded our children into mini sales representatives for the corporations, while preparing them for excessive spending, and thus, debt in the future.

The sad thing is that they are growing up in a culture of consumerism, while the values of human relationships, self-respect, discipline and charity are put on the back burner to learn later ... maybe.

**Exercise Tips for Dealing with The Nag Factor**

1. **Do you give into the "nag factor"?**
2. **How will this lack of discipline affect your children's future?**
3. **There is an amazing book on raising children titled *Kids Are Worth It by Barbara Coloroso*. Read, learn and implement the principles Ms. Coloroso teaches.**

# FINANCIAL SUCCESS : IT'S ALL IN YOUR HEAD

In the animated family movie *Megamind,* Will Ferrell plays a self-proclaimed super-intelligent, incredibly handsome criminal genius and master of all villainy. His purpose in life is to battle his nemesis, Metro Man, played by Brad Pitt, who epitomizes society's image of a real superhero. In essence, Megamind and Metro Man are complete opposites.

Metro Man turns everything he touches into success, as seen by the citizens of Earth, while Megamind's strategies and plans are turned upside down and usually result in his own physical suffering and ridicule by society. However, when Megamind was just eight days old, his parents sent him to Earth with the affirmation that he was destined for great things.

This affirmation was the premise of Megamind's persistence towards his life goal: to defeat Metro Man! Megamind eventually succeeded, but not without repeated failure and ridicule. He continually told himself that he was a genius and a superhero in a villainous kind of way.

Although *Megamind* is a family animated movie, there are some very important human lessons here. It turns out that Megamind's constant mental persistence for accomplishing a goal eventually brought Megamind the success he sought. He remained open to the idea that he had extraordinary ability, and it came to fruition. In reality, these same principles are at play for you and me.

Whatever your financial circumstances, neurons associated with old habits helped to create the results you have been getting out of life thus far. In other words, we are the source of self-sabotage through of what Anthony Robbins calls "mixed neuro-associations." Have you ever been in the situation where things are just starting to go your way but you mentally question why things are so easy and wonder why things aren't going wrong?

When we send out mixed thoughts, we'll see mixed results! This is created by the neuro-associations we have. Let me explain.

According to Anthony Robbins, the author of *Awaken the Giant Within*, when we experience a significant amount of pain or pleasure, our brain searches for the cause by enlisting a three-step process.

One. Your brain is looking for uniqueness. What stands out that is different in this situation?

Two. Your brain is looking for something that is happening at the same time as something else. What is happening right now or close to the moment must be the cause of this pain or pleasure sensation, right?

Three. Your brain is looking for something consistent. What seems to be the common theme when I feel these sensations?

Although this may seem like our brains are in complete control, they often misinterpret the inputs at each of the process stages. The example most often seen is in the area of our finances.

Let's look at an example. Most of us have spent numerous dollars on what I like to call "material trap toys." Things such as the biggest flat screen tvs, the most luxurious car or the fastest ATV. These are material things that do not enhance our life's purpose in most circumstances. When I speak with most people, what they are really looking for is freedom. For some, it's freedom from debt; for others, it is the freedom to meet their retirement goals. Still others want a balance of many things, but few ever state that their goals in life are to purchase "things." Rather, they want to fulfill their way of life!

However, when I look at what those same people spend their money on, I find that those who have the most "material trap toys" are the first ones to dwell on and procrastinate about the debt that they have accumulated. Consequently, their true life goals are not aligned with their actions. The result: Mixed Neuro-Asssociations.

An example is a person who wants to refinance her mortgage to get ahead by lowering interest costs and increasing cash flow, but then she goes out and buys a bigger car. Why?

One guess is that her brain has deep-rooted, mixed neuro-associations that are subconsciously telling her that to become rich means to have more things – more material goods, such as bigger TVs, spacious homes and newer cars. There must be a deep-rooted association that believes paying down debt is boring and not "flashy" enough to be considered rich or successful. In essence, she may need to have the lifestyle of a rich person now in order to feel accepted, regardless of whether she has the money or not. The most dangerous part of her thinking process is that it is subconscious – she doesn't even know it's going on in her head.

Another guess could be that she feels bad about having too much money. Having more money than she needs could give her the feeling that she hasn't worked hard enough to earn that extra money. When her debts are consolidated and life is beginning to look easier, she sabotages herself by acquiring more debt without ever realizing it until it is time to consolidate again.

The underlying causes to these scenarios are:

*Lack of awareness to question why she does what she does*

*Unconscious self-sabotaging habits*

In order for you to transcend your negative and self-limiting neuro-associations, you need to create new habits and methods of thinking – new habits that associate great pleasure to sculpting our life goals, new habits that force you to plan how you're going to get out of debt quicker and new habits within a new banking structure that keeps your spending habits in check by making you aware of where your money is going.

These new habits will create *new* neuro-associations, which lead to *new* behaviors and ultimately to new results.

I often contemplate why our society has become obsessed with possessions that divert money from our retirement goals and our ability to live debt-free. Over a few years, I studied exactly why I spent money the way I did. My studies led me to an interesting chemical in our brains that helps us feel good while spending money. In the next chapter, we'll discuss this addictive chemical reaction in our brains so that we can understand that we are hardwired for over-spending if we are unconscious about our habits.

By the way, if you haven't watched the movie *Megamind*, watch it. It will not only teach you lessons about persistence and confidence, it also addresses the notion of true happiness and purpose.

**Watch Your Mouth Too!**

The two most costly words you'll ever say are the words *"only"* and *"just." It's only $2 or it's just under $30.* Either way, $100,000 is made up of one million dimes or ten million pennies – money is money. Don't lose perspective of your purchasing decisions by justifying what you bought with the words "only" or "just." When you spend money, you're spending money – period! The choice had nothing to do with anything else other than that you chose to spend. The only other option would have been not to spend. Keep your decisions to purchase or not very blunt and clear.

*The secret of success is learning how to use pain and pleasure instead of having pain and pleasure use you. If you do that, you're in control of your life. If you don't, life controls you.* - Anthony Robbins in Awaken the Giant Within

Questions For Self-Examination

1. **What associations do you have about money and debt?**
2. **What did your family teach you about money and debt growing up?**
3. **Do you have perceptions, whether conscious or unconscious, that could be holding you back from debt-freedom?**
4. **What habits could you form right now to help overcome self-sabotage?**

# MORE CHOICE MEANS
# MORE SPENDING

In a world driven by consumers, it's no wonder that we demand more choice. It's common sense that if we're going to spend our hard-earned money on something, we want the confidence of knowing that we have many choices from which to make an educated decision. Or is it?

The reality is that the part of the brain that controls our ability to be rational is the same part that controls our memory. In the words of Jonah Lehrer in the book *How We Decide,* "a mind trying to remember lots of information is less able to exert control over its impulses." (p.151)

George Miller, a psychologist, concluded in his paper titled "*The Magical Number Seven, Plus or Minus Two*" that the brain can only handle approximately seven pieces of information, "plus or minus two," at any given time. Further research and experimentation by Baba Shiv and Alexander Fedorikhin confirmed in 1999 that subjects who were asked to memorize a seven-digit number were more likely to choose chocolate cake over fruit salad when compared to subjects who were asked to memorize just 1 or 2 digits.

When the brain's capacity for memorizing becomes utilized to its fullest degree, the more likely you are to make an impulsive decision. This revelation explains some purchasing decisions and could be a contributing factor to why our continent is debt-laden. The objective you should have as a consumer is to simplify your choices (to less than seven, of course) as much as possible, allowing you to make a rational decision while using your intuition as a guide. Cognitive overload can be the root cause of most of our impulsive decisions in life. The more "things" that occupy your mind, the less resolve and energy you have to be accountable to your life's goals.

# WE ARE ALL ADDICTED
# TO THE DOPE!

**Scenario A: Which would you rather have: $50 today or $55 in one week?**

I asked my daughter this very question, and her response was that if she could have the $50 today, she'd take it because if she waited two weeks for $5 extra, who knows if the desire to buy the object for which the money would be used in a week would exist.

Her statement reflects what most people would do according to a 1981 study by economist Richard Thaler. He gave subjects the choice of receiving $15 today and some higher amount in the future, and then they told him what that amount needed to be in one month, one year and ten years from today in order to motivate them to wait.

**Scenario B: Would you rather have $50 in six weeks or $55 in seven weeks?**

When made the same offer but with the added condition of waiting six weeks or seven weeks, my daughter opted for the $55 because, in her words, "You just have to wait one more week (than the six she already waited), and you get five extra dollars."

When examining scenario A, waiting a week for an extra $5 is not really worth it when we can have the money *now*. But compare that to already waiting six weeks, and the seventh week seems easier to accept for the extra money. Having $50 today is more appealing than waiting two weeks for an extra $5, but having $55 in seven weeks after waiting six weeks becomes acceptable. Why?

In the book *The Mind of The Market* by Michael Shermer, instant gratification versus delay of gratification is the main culprit in how people choose in this experiment. You see, when you experience immediate gratification, the limbic system, a region of the brain, lights up. This area is directly associated with the part of the brain that releases dopamine, a chemical "well known to be involved in drug addiction and impulsive behavior." Oh yeah, even orgasms.

Shermer also noted, *"The low-road brain structures, available in all mammals and primates, give us all the default decision of impulsivity and immediate gratification."*

Does this mean we can't control ourselves? Unconsciously, yes, but letting a primal part of our brain make impulsive decisions about spending can be retrained. Each and every time you get what you want, a chemical called *dopamine* flushes your brain, resulting in a euphoric, good feeling. The problem is that the brain is looking for more release of dopamine, but *if* you only feel good when you're shopping, the brain is being trained to release the dopamine only then. This explains why someone who buys a new car feels great for about a week or two but then goes through "buyer's remorse" once the first payment for the car loan is due.

We have created bad habits in spending, partly due to our inability to recognize that we feel good when immediately getting what we want. In the thousands of commercials we see and hear on a daily basis, I find it ironic that "feeling good" is mostly associated with buying things. Could the media be appealing to a primal part of our brains on purpose? Is the accumulation of debt just an animalistic impulse devoid of higher intellectual thinking? Is it possible to retrain our brains to feel good about our goals and our relationships?

The great news is that dopamine is a good chemical in our brains. The problem is when dopamine is associated with self-sabotaging habits that result in debt and over-consumption. It is possible to restructure our finances and methods of thinking so that we use dopamine to our advantage instead of giving that power to the companies that try to sell their products and services to you.

*When dopamine circuits go awry, addiction can result: basically an addict's dopamine circuits become so inured to the pleasures of alcohol, shopping, or opiates that he requires more and more of the substance or activity to derive the same kick.* - Sharon Begley, paraphrasing Mike Merzenich, in Train Your Mind, Change Your Brain

## The dope's not all bad

I want to take a moment to explain that dopamine is not all bad. In fact, dopamine is used by our brains for many amazing and healthy purposes, such as the regulation of all of our emotions – happiness, love and even our distaste for things.

Ever have "that gut feeling" about something? That's when dopamine does its best work. It has processed enormous amounts of data based on your experiences, both bad and good, and triggers an emotion when confronted with a decision. The challenge is to know when that emotion is telling you something and exactly what it is telling you.

### Blame it on the monkeys!

When a neuroscientist named Wolfram Schultz became obsessed about discovering the contributors in the neural system to Parkinson's disease, he used monkeys and recorded the data from the cells in their brains. His goal was to find a link between the cells and the body's movements, but he failed to do so.

What Schultz noticed after many years of research was that the dopamine neurons in the monkeys seemed to fire just before he gave a monkey a reward in the form of a banana. He then decided to conduct experiments that would seek to reveal how a dopamine neuron could process so much information.

The experiment involved sounding a loud tone and then giving the monkey a squirt of juice. Initially, the monkeys' dopamine neurons would fire when the reward was given. It didn't take long, though, when the monkey's neurons were responding to the tone, and if it received the reward, a surge of dopamine was released to the brain. However, if the tone sounded and no reward was given, the dopamine neurons seemed to fire less because they predicted a reward and received nothing. Basically, the dopamine neurons were acting as "prediction neurons," signaling whether the prediction was successful or in error.

Our dopamine neurons work exactly the same way. Experiences allow our dopamine neurons to predict outcomes, and when we're right about our expectations, we feel a surge of ecstasy. On the other hand, when we're wrong about our predictions and expectations, we store that disappointment and recalibrate our future expectations.

This is why experts in success coaching stress that we must learn from our mistakes by accepting the outcome and using it as fuel to become better. If you look at the positive lesson in the most negative of outcomes, your dopamine neurons are storing positive data for use in future decisions, such as buying a new home, a car and getting into debt! On the contrary, if we make a mistake and simply dwell on the negativity of the circumstance, all we're training our neurons to do is respond negatively to a similar situation in the future, thus limiting our potential, our success and our happiness.

As I did the research for this book, I was amazed at how much interrelated information exists on the concepts of money, debt and success. One such piece of information came from leadership expert John Maxwell in his book *Success 101*. The lesson I learned from reading his book was that most of us who desire success and happiness are really focused on *becoming* and not *being*. In other words, we make financial decisions that get us into debt because we think that we'll relish the benefits of *being* what we desire, when all that is energizing our souls is the *becoming* of what we desire. After we get what we want, we realize that our decisions and their consequences were not really what we had expected.

### Nothing can get you into debt faster than surprise!

Remember Wolfram Schultz's monkey experiment? Although he discovered that dopamine neurons fire when they can predict the reward, he also uncovered that they fire even more when they were surprised. When the monkeys heard the tone, received the juice, but then encountered a surprise squirt of juice without the sound of the tone, their neurons fired like never before. As Jonah Leher paraphrases this phenomena in the book *How We Decide,* "The purpose of this dopamine surge is to make the brain pay attention to new, and potentially important stimuli." The dilemma is that you have to figure out what is "potentially important."

It makes perfect sense why every single infomercial on TV does their best to offer you their product, but at the end they "surprise" us by offering a free gift or a duplicate of the product for no extra cost. Clearly, big business knows about the surprise affect on your brain. Even credit card companies play this game by offering you a "free" gift with a credit card application. Even still, it is very common for mortgage companies, such as CIBC's (Canadian Imperial Bank of Commerce) PC Financial, to surprise you with grocery points when you fund a new mortgage with them. Society is littered with "surprise" offers, just like a lone fish in a pond with a thousand hooks and a surprise worm on each one! This also explains why some women love being surprised by flowers and men with an unanticipated win at the poker table.

Every time we make a purchase or conduct a financial decision which is then accompanied by a pleasant surprise, we run the risk of letting our dopamine neurons get the best of us by releasing a surge of chemical bliss to our brains. Once you truly understand this method of coaxing and convincing us to spend and how our brains react, you can then master the temptation to spend unnecessarily.

**Exercise your neural system: The Dopamine Exercise**

Now that you have a basic understanding of the dopamine system, let's take some time and practice to retrain those neurons.

1. Delay Instant Gratification

One of the most powerful things you can do to retrain your dopamine neurons is to delay instant gratification. Sure, we want things, but the next time you're tempted to buy something such as a piece of clothing, pick it up, try it on, smell it, etc., ***but put it*** *back on the hanger and leave!* Go buy a coffee or tea (something of much lesser value), and go for a walk.

When making a decision to purchase a product, ask yourself this question:

*Will making this purchase truly change my life?*

You will notice that most of your temptation to buy things does not enhance your life, and you won't die if you don't get it!

2. Pull out a piece of paper and draw a line through the middle of it vertically. Now, write down all of the things in your life for which you are thankful in one column. This list may include, but is not limited to children, spouse, sunshine, food, health, savings, house, etc. Your list of things you are grateful can be limitless.

Once you have your list in column one, write a brief reason as to *why* you are so thankful for that item or person in column two. Taking time to be thankful and truly feeling it will create a surge of dopamine in your system, giving you an appreciation for the true essence of your life, instead of the material world. This exercise should be done on a regular basis until you instill the habit of being grateful for what you do have.

# BUYING A HOME? FIRST SHOP FOR STRAWBERRY JAM!

When I read a 1985 article from the *The Pittsburg Press* about a *Consumer Reports* study on strawberry jam, I could not help seeing a relationship between how we buy jam and how we buy homes.

*Huh?*

That's right, the neurological processes that occur when you buy strawberry jam are the very same ones that will tell you whether you are buying the right home or not. The problem is that you would never realize this unless you knew how our brains process this information and how they reveal the answers to us through an emotional response. The key is to develop the ability to read your own emotions and you will end up buying the right home!

When *Consumer Reports* hired the very best food technologist and sensory consultants, they had rated 44 jam varieties and published their results. When Timothy Wilson and Pittsburgh researcher Jonathan Schooler decided to replicate this taste test with "non-experts," the "non-experts" ranked the jams in a similar order as the experts had ranked them. However, when the experiment was performed again, the researchers asked the subjects "why?" they were choosing what they were choosing, and the jam rankings dramatically differed. The tasters in the second run of the experiment were forced to explain a decision which is usually impulsive, not rational.

"Rationalization" or "thinking things through" is embraced in North American culture as a "wise thing" to do, but based on the results of this strawberry jam taste test, more thinking and rationalizing one's choices led to choosing the worst ranked jams! It turns out that we can justify even the worst products and services if we over-think the choices.

This is not the only experiment that supports these results. Studies on cheap versus expensive wines and cheap art versus expensive art all lead to the same result – that over analyzing your choices leads to the worst choices.

The "placebo effect" is to blame in all of these situations. When your brain has the *expectation* of something, it will work to reframe your choice to support your decision, even if it's the wrong one.

There are two parts of your brain that can kick in when making a buying decision: the prefrontal cortex and the limbic system. The prefrontal cortex processes logic and rational thought, while the limbic system manages all of your emotional responses, both conscious and unconscious. Keep in mind that this is a very general explanation for the purposes of understanding how we make buying decision.

The limbic system is what kicks in when an airline pilot makes a split second decision to avert a plane crash or when an FBI agent decides to shoot in a hostage situation, and it even plays a role in the decision to purchase strawberry jam. Essentially, all of these choices are difficult to explain through rational thought, yet all of them involve the use of our intuition. Our intuitive choices are patterns that our brains have developed based on past expectations and the results of those expectations. The more experiences you go through, the more your brain is able to register intuitive responses to those situations when they come up again. Each time an expectation turns out to be false, your brain adjusts its intuitive capabilities so that when this situation comes up again in the future, it is ready to trigger an emotional response.

Ever have that feeling that something was not right? That's your emotional brain telling you the answer based on a past experience. The challenge is to decode what exactly is "wrong" by understanding your emotions.

Your brain will tell you when you have found the right home, but it is all too easy to rationalize your purchase before giving your brain the tools and sensory inputs it needs to tell you what is right for you. Home builders know this when they make their model homes look great or when home stagers make a home look perfect! Our brains will fall in love with the look of a home, and then we'll justify that feeling by rationalizing all the reasons we should buy that home. Meanwhile, your emotional brain may be telling you that it is a far commute from and to work, that the builder's reputation is not the best, that you will have to spend money after the closing on a fence, deck or shed, and the list can go on and on. I am not against buying a new home, but I wanted to use this as a classic example of how rationalizing a purchase can block out essential costs and factors when buying a new home.

*So how do you give your brain the right sensory inputs?*

The best and most effective way to give your emotional brain the right inputs is to give it more experiences from which it can draw subconscious conclusions in order to help you decide, should you choose to tap into those emotions. Go out and see as many homes as you can! Take your time in each home, developing a sense of likes and dislikes, without justifying each. Do this over several weeks so that you are not relying on "excitement" to make a decision *(excitement is related to the chemical known as dopamine, which was covered in the last chapter).* I also urge you to make a list of "must have" and "absolutely not." When you visit each house, become attuned to your list and make notes as they relate to your list. Intuitively, your emotional brain will develop a sense for what you want and trigger a positive feeling or a negative one as you visit more homes.

The next time you stop by the grocery store to pick up some strawberry jam, appreciate the fact that your brain can help you pick the best tasting (emotional) one, or you might choose the one that tastes the worst but meets all seemingly logical criteria for choosing jam (rational). It may save you from making a bigger mistake, like buying a home for the wrong reasons!

# MEET INSULA: DISGUSTINGLY DEBT-FREE!

It's ironic that an experiment examining how subjects make purchases and their reactions to the prices of those purchases was named SHOP – the *Save Holdings or Purchase* experiment by Stanford University neuroscientist Brian Knutson.

Subjects were given the choice of buying a box of Godiva® chocolates or a DVD of the Simpsons television series. Four seconds after each was shown, the price was unveiled to each subject. Four seconds after that a button was given to each subject to choose if they wanted to make a purchase.

The buttons were mixed around so that any preferences to choose left versus right was eliminated. Some purchases were not real while others were given $20 to spend on the displayed items.

When a product appears, it stimulates the middle of the brain or that area I spoke about in the previous chapter associated with the reward or gratification function in our brains. This part of the brain is also involved in evaluating things. When the price of the product appeared, it activated a region of the brain that is linked to higher uses and decisions. Finally, when the scientists mixed up the data so

NUEROTIC MONEY

that they could analyze the difference between the price of a product and what they were willing to pay, they found that an area of the brain called the *insula* lit up.

The Insula is brought to life when experiencing negative stimulai such as bad smells. Interestingly, the insula became particularly active when the subject decided NOT to make the purchase. When the subject experienced a level of disgust from a price perceived as too high, the insula kicked in and prevented the purchase.

Amazingly, dopamine convinces us to spend money with the goal of instant gratification, but the sophisticated human brain has a mechanism called the insula that can override the more primitive part of the brain, and they're right beside each other! When the insula is activated, it releases a chemical *noradrenaline* which is thought to be linked to fear and anxiety. We need to teach the insula and the chemical dopamine to switch their roles in our brains if we are to overcome debt.

How do we use insula to protect our financial goals and plans? How can we overcome the primitive parts of our brain that contribute to instant gratification and help the higher and more sophisticated parts of the brain learn to disgust such activity before the dopamine kicks in?

We have conditioned ourselves to unconsciously overspend because of our bad habits – the need to "feel good" now – and we lack financial discipline. An overwhelming number of North Americans can only *hope* to be debt-free some day.

We can reverse the functions of dopamine and the insula. It's as if we need to smell the stench of bad debt first in order to trigger disgust about the way we are doing things. We need to introduce the orgasmic pleasure chemical (dopamine) when we follow our financial plan, not when we buy a TV or a new car. It is possible to start feeling really good about your long-term financial goals instead of a new pair of Nikes®.

It's amazing that the same part of our brain that is linked to sex is the same one linked to spending. Most of us think twice about acting out on the sexual impulses from within, but we let that same part of the brain lose control when it comes to getting into debt. Could it be that the *perceived* future consequences of impulsive sex are greater than the perceived consequences of purchases made on credit? Back in the first chapter, we learned about how money is created – that it is magical and constantly changing. It can be concluded that the consequences of money are just too complicated for the primal part of the brain to intuitively understand, and that's just how the banks want it!

*"... sex and shopping are not so far apart, particularly in the brain, and we would be well advised to listen to the whisperings from within of what those feelings are trying to tell us about the possible consequences of our actions."* - Michael Shermer, The Mind and The Market

Bringing this knowledge about fear, anxiety and disgust to our consciousness while consciously acknowledging that we tend to feel good about spending will help you achieve your financial goals, including being completely debt-free.

Self-Examination Exercise

Let's get your insula working *for* you, not against you! I want you to sit and close your eyes for a moment after reading the rest of this exercise. I want you to read the following scenario and then close your eyes and really envision what the following would feel like as if it were happening today! If you can, get someone else to read this to you while you relax and really visualize.

- Imagine you are ten years older than today. What does that feel like? How does your body feel? Where are you working?

- You have aged ten years, but your debt has remained the same for those ten years. It may even have gone up since ten years ago. You thought that you'd be closer to retirement or even just debt-free, but you squandered your cash-flow on things you thought you needed ten years earlier.

- How does it feel to have accumulated more debt for a new car? Was it worth it to move into a larger home when your debt wasn't paid down? How's your credit card balance?

- Do you feel trapped? Like you've wasted ten years?

- What if you had died today and could see your funeral? How would your financial legacy be felt? Would you have enough assets to pay off your debts so that they weren't a burden for your family? Would you have anything left for your family? Would your death be a burden on the family's finances? How does that feel?

- Take a deep breath in and visualize all of the habits, thoughts and actions you must develop to become debt-free in ten years. When you exhale, let out all of the mental garbage associated with getting into debt. When you breathe in, visualize attracting more money than you need, and when you breathe out, visualize letting go of all temptations to spend money foolishly. Breathe ten times. Open your eyes.

What you've done in this visualization, you have engaged the insula to feel disgusted with being in debt as if it were happening today. The more you can engage the feeling of disgust with spending money you don't yet have, the better decisions you can make for your finances going forward.

# PUTTING IT ALL TOGETHER

Since chapter one, we've explored the evolution of money as we know it today. We accept that money will always change. We have also learned that the money system is complicated and that having debt increases our risk of financial meltdown. We've touched on how our culture and attitude reflect our debt, and we've discussed the effects our children and our brains have on our buying decisions. So, now what do you do?

In the following chapters, I'll give you advice from my former careers as a mortgage broker and banker. I will also give some advice as a borrower and a reader. You'll read about your biggest debt, your mortgage, and then you'll be given a list of really good resources to further quench your thirst for debt freedom.

I don't know all of the answers, but I have one: my answer. Enjoy!

# HOW TO GET OUT

**Warning!**

The following chapters are dedicated to getting out of debt, but they are based completely on my experiences as a banker, a mortgage broker, a family man and a reader with an appetite for knowledge. Some of these strategies for getting out of debt and curtailing spending are controversial and may not sit well with traditional financial planners, bankers and mortgage brokers, but I want you, the consumer, to be armed with enough information to ask critical questions to these professionals.

In my observations over the years, many of the financial planners, bankers and mortgage brokers who serve customers everyday are in debt, have gone bankrupt at one time or another, or they are lousy savers themselves. How do I know? I worked with them, and I was one of those lousy savers. Everything that helped me start saving money and get out of debt came from trusting my intuition and experience, not tradition. I want you to use caution and figure out what is right for your particular situation, not mine, not your banker's and not for your planner's benefit.

Remember, nobody will take care of you better than you! It starts now, and I support your efforts to achieve debt freedom and financial prosperity.

# TAKE A PICTURE – TAKE A LIFESTYLE SNAPSHOT!

Christine and Mike were your typical middleclass family with three children. Mike worked as a professor, teaching (of all things) human behaviour, and Christine worked in the healthcare field. By traditional standards, both made "good" money, had beautiful children, lived in a new home and seemed happy enough.

When Christine requested an interview to review her mortgage, my first thought was that it was up for renewal or they wanted additional money, both of which were common transactions for a family like hers. When I arrived at Christine's house, I was greeted by an excited 3-year-old son and her husband Mike with smiles that revealed a slight nervousness, yet a relief that I was there. We proceeded to the kitchen table.

One of the first questions I asked was where they'd like to be as a family in three years, and that's when Christine broke down and let out every frustration with their money situation.

*"We have too much debt; it's building up, not going down, and we need serious help!"*

I was caught off guard that Christine's situation seemed so dire to her based on their outward appearances in public. However, I was not surprised at their debt levels and their worry. You see, most middle class and high income earning families have too much debt, yet they refuse to admit it. Fortunately for Christine, she couldn't take any more of the stress associated with worrying about their debt. What followed from Christine's mouth was a typical response of those in such denial, *"We track all of our expenses, and I'm careful about what we spend, but it seems like we can't make it work. Are we going to go bankrupt?"*

Most people make a "budget" – a one time piece of paper with categories for different expenses based on their "perception" of what those expenses are. In reality, most people don't have a clue what things cost them. First, the human brain can only compute an average of seven things at any one time. With children running array, functions to attend and at least seven different bills needing to be paid at any one time, most people are simply confused about their expenses. Second, and more importantly, most debts, bills and expenses are paid by automatic debit, internet banking and plastic, such as a credit card or debit card; keeping track of these expenses is often chaotic and cumbersome.

Christine and Mike were no different. I had them prepare a superficial expense sheet that I like to call *Your Lifestyle Snapshot*™. Simply by changing the name to "Lifestyle Snapshot," the client's brain shifts from the negative perceptions of a budget to a mindset that seeks to identify the facts, not the expectations of a budget. We went through each category, one by one. As I confirmed each expense, I ripped it apart by asking Christine and Mike to pull out their bank statements to confirm the expense. Some expenses were overstated, while some were grossly understated or even forgotten until we unburied them in last September's bank statement. One of the most fascinating discoveries was the fact that Christine grossly underestimated her own income! What seemed like a horizon of bankruptcy and foreclosure turned into a spectacular sunrise for Christine as she realized that she had more money than she had originally realized. This gave us both opportunity and hope.

A *Lifestyle Snapshot*™ is an expanded budget sheet that captures not only your core expenses, such as mortgage payment, property taxes and utilities, but also encapsulates the little expenses – our indulgences, such as coffee, alcohol, cigarettes, gym memberships and eating out.

Before filling out the Lifestyle Snapshot, each client was put through The 30-Day Track™, whereby a calendar is placed in a conspicuous place at home, such as a coffee table, refrigerator or kitchen countertop, and each time you spend money, it gets written down and tracked for that day. At the end of 30 days, you take the data from The 30-Day Track AND your bank statement and proceed to complete the Lifestyle Snapshot.

What I found by having clients track their expenses for 30 days was not only that they realized exactly where their money was going, but their attitude toward frivolous spending shifted just by doing the exercise. Most clients said that they began to spend "consciously" and with "purpose," whereas prior to tracking, they'd spend without thinking.

There is a magical benefit to tracking your expenses. Moreover, not tracking is like playing the final of The Stanley Cup without keeping score! You can't win the game if you're not keeping score.

Both The Lifestyle Snapshot™ and The 30-Day Track™ can be downloaded by contacting me at joeornato@me.com.

# YOUR HOME (OR HOUSE)

A "home" is a house that has meaning to its inhabitants, while a "house" is just its physical structure with no emotional attachment to it. The problem is that most of us would like to think of our dwellings as "homes," but let's look at our places as "houses" for a minute in order to conclude that a *home* or a *house* costs us money either way you look at it.

It was January of 1996 when Maggie and I began looking for our first house. I proposed to Maggie during the previous Autumn, and our wedding date was set for October of 1996. The traditional thing to do once one got married (or so we thought) was to purchase a home. Our parents had drilled the concept that rent was a bad thing, wasted money, while a home was an investment for the long run. I worked for a couple of years at a major Canadian bank while Maggie was building a successful clientele as a hair stylist.

After a few weeks of constant searching, we finally stumbled on a new subdivision in South London that offered us a builder's "spec" home, and we'd get to choose the interior colours, carpeting, etc. We were thrilled and didn't think twice about arranging the purchase, our mortgage and our move-in date.

It was a small home with less than 1200 square feet of living space on a zero lot line property that had just enough of a yard for a small garden, a deck and some fruit trees. It was located in a cul-de-sac with a street that was too small for the amount of cars everyone owned. In fact, when someone parked their car on the road, it was difficult to back out of the driveway without the threat of causing a fender bender!

The home cost us $125,000, the property taxes were $1900 per year, the heating bill was less than $100 per month, as well as the electricity bill. The expenses were very manageable, and our incomes were growing. Meanwhile, God blessed us with our first child, Julia. When we found out we were expecting our second child in 2001, we convinced ourselves that our three-bedroom home was not large enough for a family of four, so we moved a bit more east to a new, master-planned subdivision named Summerside.

Again, we decided to purchase a brand new home. Our four-level back-split cost us $190,000 in 2001 on a lot that was a few feet bigger than our previous home. Property taxes increased to $2800 per year, and the heating and electrical bills both went up as well. It was okay though. We justified the extra expenses with more space for our family and entertaining and the fact that, by then, I was a successful mortgage broker and Maggie had a full clientele. Our home in Summerside helped us build a home-based mortgage practice and a hair salon, both on different levels. The money became so good that eating out was a regular habit. Our home's decorating changed as often as the shelves at Homesense! Again, the itch that we needed more kicked in. We scratched that itch by deciding to build a 3200-square-foot home on another cul-de-sac in Summerside that was worth $425,000.

Our Bellsmith Court home was what we needed to grow my mortgage business – there was room for me to have an assistant, while Maggie's salon could be more inviting at the main entrance of the home. Everything at Bellsmith Court was bigger than we had ever had, including the expenses. Property taxes went to over $6000 per year heating cost us $150 per month, and electricity went to an average of $250 per month. Three or four years went by, and we realized how stressful it was to have two businesses at home, so I moved my mortgage practice to the local plaza. With this added peace of mind at home, without the phone ringing every few minutes, Maggie and I contemplated the history of our choices.

We concluded that our decisions for spending more and more money were fuelled not by the need for space for a growing family or business but by the expectation that a new home would make us more happy than we were. Upon digging deeper, we also realized that our purchases reflected a desire to be viewed as successful by society – by our parents, our relatives, our friends and our clients.

The way we figured this out was by vacationing – getting away from everyday life in order to reflect. Maggie and I are known among our family and friends as adventurers. We often avoid the tourist destinations and embrace local culture wherever we go. When visiting Nashville, we'd stay in a small cabin at an 80-acre farm outside the city and even attend musicals at local middle schools. In Phoenix, we'd rent a condo in the middle of a predominantly South American neighbourhood. Finally, in Portugal, we stay at Maggie's parents' 1960s home that has no heat, no cooling, no gas water heater and is located in a fishing village.

During each and every one of our vacations, we had the opportunity to live with less, and we enjoyed it. We discovered that our happiness was in everyday living, not in chasing material things. Every time we came back from vacation, we'd instill a piece of what we learned into our everyday lives. We learned that a home is any place that you can enjoy eating and drinking with family and friends, as well as a safe place to sleep or simply sit in peace. A house, on the other hand, is the cost associated with living in a home. A house does not make the home – the people do!

In Europe, it was tradition for families to live in close villages, often sharing their properties and homes with their children so that everyone could live cost-effectively. Helping one another is second nature to Europeans. Once their children have saved enough money to purchase their own home or car, they do it with savings and minimal debt.

Recently, the issue of governments defaulting on debt in Europe is dominating the news. My recent trip to Portugal in October of 2011 revealed to me the following about European financial culture:
1. Only recently did young European adults become comfortable with borrowing money to buy things.
2. Prior to borrowing, young European adults saved and/or lived together with their relatives. Property was inherited and kept in the family.
3. With the recent European meltdown, young European adults simply turned their mortgaged homes and cars over to the banks and went back to living with their relatives. They still go to the cafes several times a day. They still have a cell phone, a computer and a car. They seem to have enough money for the things they need daily.
4. The media in Europe has convinced the public that there is an economic crisis, but the actions of the public reflect life as it was before this debt mentality made its way into the European culture.

In contrast, North Americans have enormous pride and consider it a failure to depend on others, so we go and buy our homes, cars, TVs, etc. on our own, meaning without depending on our parents, family and friends. Unfortunately, we North Americans do not make these purchases with savings either – we borrow. We often envy the Europeans' lifestyle with statements such as, "*Europeans work to live. North Americans live to work.*" Could it be that our desire to want things instantaneously contributes to our debt load? Debt propels us into fast-paced living. We borrow now for things we should wait to buy in the future.

Now, I can see investment advisors, bankers and mortgage brokers condemning me for shunning the idea of borrowing to make investments. Should you borrow to buy a home or save the money? Should you borrow to buy a car or save the money? Should you borrow to buy Christmas presents or save the money? Sure, saving the money would be ideal, but buying a home with saved money would take decades for most people. So what do you do?

One of the biggest mistakes I ever made when buying or building a home was thinking that it was an investment. A house is not an investment unless it produces income to cover your costs of owning it – period! Anyone who thinks that any house is an investment is just being fooled by the banker who needs your mortgage; you're being tricked by the real estate agent who needs your commission; you're being sold by the insurance agent who needs your policy; and you're being bled by the government who needs your property taxes! When a house costs you money, it is a liability, not an investment.

To overcome the costs of owning a home, it is advisable to explore the opportunities of earning income from it. As a first time buyer, I was never taught that one of the best investment decisions I could have ever made was to buy a duplex or a tri-plex and live in one of the units. Not only would this decision have given me income to cover the costs of home ownership, it would have taught me managerial skills and conflict management skills in my early twenties that are invaluable when you grow older. Sure, there will be difficulties from time to time when owning an income property, but these challenges are nowhere near the stress of having a house cost you money each and every day, without the possibility of putting you in the black until you sell that home twenty or thirty years in the future, supposing that there isn't a market meltdown in real estate by then.

# YOUR MORTGAGE

Most of us who ever purchase a home will require a mortgage to do so. Although I have shunned debt overall, I do understand that a mortgage is probably inevitable at some point in your life. I have held several mortgages, and those mortgages translated into life knowledge (often through hard knocks). That being said, if you employ the mindset of the last chapter – that a home is not an investment unless it makes you money – you can justify the mortgage as a way to help you live more efficiently than by renting.

This chapter will give an overview of the current mortgage market in Canada, as well as what you can do as a consumer to make efficient choices when shopping for a mortgage. Actually, I hate the word "shopping" when it is associated with mortgages because it understates the impact of this massive debt. A mortgage is a financial anchor. It allows you to make a really, really big purchase today with money that you haven't yet made and plan to pay over the next two or three decades! That's not something to "shop" for – it's something to be studied!

My experiences as both a banker and a mortgage broker will be revealed in this chapter, but I will combine those experiences with the ones I had as a consumer, a father and a husband. Debt affects all aspects of our lives, whether professional or social.

## Interest Rate

One of the first things that comes to mind when selecting a mortgage is the interest rate. On every street corner with a bank, you'll find either a billboard or a poster that offers a competitive interest rate. I would like to balk in the face of tradition and tell you that interest rate is NOT the determining factor in selecting the right mortgage. In fact, it is third or fourth on the priority list. Don't believe me? Take a look at a $200,000 mortgage at a rate of 4% compounded semi-annually. The interest will cost you $37,230.00 over 5 years. Take that same rate but compound it monthly, such as is the case with a line of credit, and the interest will cost you $37,549.65. On the surface, the same interest rate should cost the same in terms of dollars, but one subtle change in "the fine print" can cost you an additional $319.65 over the next 5 years. Okay big deal, an extra $319.65 is not much money, but if a mortgage company is able to change the cost of a mortgage by the simple wording of compounding frequency, imagine what they can do with other aspects of your mortgage. By the way, compounding is the way a lender earns interest on top of the interest paid. Typically, mortgages do this semi-annually or twice per year, but some mortgages and lines of credit do this each month, thus increasing the overall amount of money you pay the lender over time.

## The Mortgage Secret

The banks have done a fantastic job in convincing us to accept that there are few choices when it comes to our mortgage debts. That is to say that the only real choices we have are those that pertain to interest rates and prepayment options (how often you can pay off your mortgage). However, there has been a hybrid mortgage product on the market for over a decade that receives little attention, no consideration and is pre-judged by so-called "mortgage professionals" before they have studied and weighed the benefits of such a product.

I am talking about the all-in-one style of mortgage, originally from Australia, but pioneered in Canada by Manulife Bank, known as "Manulife ONE®." The all-in-one (AIO) style of product harnesses the flexibility of a line of credit – such as using it whenever you want to – with a low variable rate interest rate, and combines those features with a bank account. Essentially, you now do your banking out of your mortgage account.

Before you judge the merits of this product based on what other "experts" have said, just try to understand that an AIO is a concept, not just a product. It changes the way you do your banking and look at banks in order to achieve a fast-paced mortgage payoff date. How do I know? I am proof! Manulife ONE® and National Bank's All-In-One® accounts helped me become debt-free in less than 10 years. Okay, back to the concept.

Let's just picture how you do your banking right now. If you're a typical household, you have a chequing account of some sort. Each payday, your income goes into your chequing account, and then you begin by spending your income on mortgage payments, utilities, groceries, et cetera. The money that remains after expenses just sits in your chequing account, or you may even transfer some to a savings account, earning a whopping 1-2% interest. *If you're a typical family, there is some, albeit it doesn't feel like much to most, left-over spending money each paycheque.* Most of us feel that we need to stockpile this extra money in case of a future emergency, such as a car repair. In essence, we create surpluses in our bank accounts out of *fear* that we may need that money sometime in the future.

What we should be doing with that extra money is lumping every single dollar we have left against our mortgage debt to become debt-free faster, but in the current banking structure, that would add additional stress to your life; if you drained your bank account to zero every payday and something DID happen unexpectedly, you'd most likely be in a financial disaster. Even if you had built up equity in your home by paying down your mortgage, if you needed that money quickly, the bank is likely to force you to pay for lawyer fees, penalties and possibly even a higher interest rate by refinancing your current mortgage contract. On top of that, you may not even qualify for additional money if your credit rating has been damaged or if the government has changed the rules for qualifying for a mortgage, as happened in Canada in 2009-2010 and now again in 2012. Only a minority of borrowers in Canada are in a position to lump extra money against their mortgage without the fear of having no funds available for emergencies. The rest of us are stuck paying a mortgage for 25 years or more and hope to refinance when emergencies come up.

Well, an AIO style mortgage combines your bank account with your mortgage debt, making it one very big overdraft attached to your bank account, but at a prime rate of interest. Each time your paycheque goes into the account, it PAYS DOWN the PRINCIPLE immediately, thereby reducing the interest associated with those funds.

Of course, you'll have the same expenses as before, such as utilities, property taxes, groceries, but the mortgage payment was the income that was deposited. This type of account does NOT ask for a blended principle and interest payment from you. Any funds that go into the account pay down your debt immediately! Right away, the interest calculated at the end of the month is reflective of what your average balance was for that month, whereas a traditional mortgage calculates its interest each and every payment based on amortizing it over 20, 25 or even 35 years! The traditional mortgage takes a fraction of each mortgage payment and allots it to the principle, while collecting a significant portion of interest.

In an AIO, you determine what the interest charge will be by the amount of extra money that remains in the account. In essence, every dollar pays down your debt until it is needed. In order to have the same affect in the traditional system, you would have had to take EVERY DOLLAR that is left over each paycheque and make a lump sum payment on your mortgage. However, in traditional banking, it's risky to do this because if you need money or forgot that a preauthorized payment was coming up, you'd be stuck with NSF (non-sufficient funds) fees by your bank for not having money in your account.

Our banks have created a banking structure based on our fears – fears that if we do not stock pile money in our chequing and savings accounts, we are asking for trouble. In an AIO, everything goes toward your debt, building equity right away. When expenses are debited, the AIO account allows those expenses to go against your equity, and only AT THAT TIME do you pay interest on that money. In the current system, you ARE PAYING INTEREST, ALWAYS, UNTIL YOU "FEEL" THAT YOU CAN AFFORD TO MAKE EXTRA PAYMENTS ON YOUR MORTGAGE. In an AIO, YOU ONLY PAY INTEREST WHEN YOU USE THE MONEY YOU NEED. It is this minor difference that allows debt freedom to arrive faster than you could have ever imagined.

Let's put an example into action.

Mario and Jen are a typical middle class family. They earn a combined income of $6500 per month after taxes (NET income or *take-home pay*). Currently, their balance sheet looks like this:

| Monthly Income: | $6500 |
|---|---|
| **Monthly Expenses:** | |
| Mortgage: | $1176.47 |
| Property taxes: | $350 |
| Utilities: | $800  (Phone, gas, water, electricity, internet, etc.) |
| Food: | $1000 |
| Entertainment: | $300 |
| Sports/Other: | $550 |
| TOTAL DISPOSABLE INCOME: | $2323.53 |

*(I have purposely left out any other debts and have assumed that Mario and Jen have none for simplicity. If you have other debts, such as credit cards and car loans, they MUST be factored in, although they could be refinanced within the AIO).*

If Mario and Jen switch to an AIO mortgage, inside which they do their banking, there is no need for a separate mortgage payment anymore because as along as the $6500 worth of income goes in each month, the lender is satisfied that the client has met their interest payment obligation. Once the $6500 is applied, their mortgage balance is immediately reduced by $6500. However, they still have expenses in the form of property taxes ($350), utilities ($800), food ($1000), entertainment ($300) and sports or other expenses amounting to $550. Their grand total of expenses WITHOUT the mortgage payment is now $3000. With $3000 of disposable income sitting against their mortgage debt every month, their mortgage goes from 25 years with a traditional payment to 5 years 10 months! Think about it - $3000 is being applied to their mortgage every single month; that's like prepaying your mortgage by $36,000 each year!

By traditional standards, this is an impossible feat for the majority of borrowers, but for an AIO client, this becomes reality – all because of efficient banking. Let's be clear here: there is NO MAGIC in this system. It is all based on addition and subtraction, but because we have been taught by our banks only one way to do our banking, they have grown the mortgage market into a $900+ billion money maker annually! [Source: CAAMP Annual State of the Residential Mortgage Market 2006-2011]

There is an old saying when it comes to warfare: "Divide and conquer." This is exactly what the banks have done with our money. They divide our payments and our bank accounts, which conquers our ability to get ahead faster. Consequently, the banks prosper more and more. When you simplify your finances, the result is clarity, purpose and prosperity.

*"If this is such a great product, then why isn't everyone doing this?"*

This is the most common objection I saw while educating my former customers about the AIO system. There are a few reasons as to why you have not heard about the AIO, and some of these reasons border on conspiracy theories, but I am going to reveal them anyway.

First, as I had stated earlier, the mortgage industry is a $900+ billion industry in Canada. Worldwide, it is in the trillions (I just heard that on BBC News during a discussion about the European debt crisis). Contrary to what most socialists think, banks exist to make profit for their shareholders, not to provide banking for the good of society. Why would any major institution offer a debt product so powerful as to reduce the profit they make on that debt by more than 50%?

Second, mortgage brokers are supposed to be working for the best interest of the customer by shopping the market for useful tools and products. How come most brokers have no experience in working with an AIO product? Simple; their commission gets in the way. You see, brokers are paid more by the banks to sell traditional mortgages, whereas the products associated with an AIO system pay as little as 40% of a full commission. On top of that, you would never need to renew your mortgage again with an AIO, so the broker is not only forfeiting profit today, but long-term profit by selling you a product that won't be needed again in less than 10 years! Moreover, most brokers have earned a form of "points" with traditional lenders, meaning that the lender buys them goods and services on a tax-free basis for sending business their way. If your mortgage was ever with a firm called CIBC®, MCAP®, Scotiabank® or ResMor Trust®, ask your broker just how their "points" system works and why they are allowed to charge a higher rate for one client and use the points to give another client a discount? I challenged my counterparts during my career to consider the AIO as an integral part in their arsenal of tools for helping clients, but every broker would simply dismiss the AIO without studying its merits.

Third, the lenders who DO offer the AIO are profiting from your AIO mortgage in one of two ways. They expect that you will not have the discipline to pay down your debt in the record time you expect, and they hope that you have more expenses than you had originally calculated. Or, they expect you to make such tremendous gains from your AIO that they want you to invest with them as you become richer.

Finally, the rules for qualifying for an AIO are pretty strict. Your credit must be impeccable, and you must have more than 25% equity in your home. That alone eliminates many potential customers.

## CAUTION

Before jumping into an AIO, it is vital that you sit with a qualified educator on the AIO to calculate your expenses, so they can be entered conservatively into the equation. When you calculate expenses, I inflate some expenses by 10% to give us a buffer, but I also inflate the interest rate on the AIO to 7% in order to compensate for rate fluctuations. 7% just happens to be the average of interest rates in Canada for the past 50 years. As I write this book, rates are in the 3-4% range. It makes no sense whatsoever to "sugar coat" your numbers in order to make a decision. The AIO should work dramatically in your favor, or DON'T DO IT AT ALL!

## Traditional Mortgages

Now it would seem that after learning the power of an all-in-one mortgage, that there is nothing left to talk about, but that's just wrong. As I said earlier, not everyone can qualify for an all-in-one, whether by credit criteria alone or because the numbers just don't make sense. Heck, some customers I have met didn't go into an all-in-one mortgage because they didn't trust themselves. If it doesn't feel right, don't do it, but continue to educate yourself about your options. Most uneasiness about financial products has to do with a lack of education rather than a scheme, so do your homework until you are confident in your decision.

The majority of readers who pick up this book will have a traditional mortgage by which you make a blended interest and principle payment over an amortization period of 10, 20, 25 or maybe even

35 years. Taking that long to pay off a mortgage seems ludicrous, but it is an accepted reality for most borrowers. However, there are many things you can do to minimize how long you take to pay off that debt and how much interest you pay as well.

The first thing you should do is *hire a trustworthy mortgage broker*. Sure, a trustworthy banker is okay too, but a banker is limited in terms of product variety on the market and is less likely to know about unique strategies outside of the bank. Furthermore, bankers are paid by the bank to achieve sales goals and meet product quotas. On the flip side, mortgage brokers are driven by commission; a trustworthy broker will consider commission secondary so that they can build a referral-based business on the hard work and honesty they display to each and every customer. Ask someone who has had a fantastic experience with a broker for a contact, and do your own interviews. A good broker will not exert pressure on you to make a quick decision.

Once the broker has helped you determine which mortgage product is right for you, it's time to start paying it back. **Pay the mortgage weekly or bi-weekly accelerated**, which means every week or every two weeks. I advocate that whatever cycle on which your paycheque arrives, make the mortgage payment that same week. Weekly or bi-weekly accelerated will cut about 5 years off the life of a 25-year amortization because twice per year, there are five weeks per month, thereby subtracting extra money from the principal of the mortgage. This is also a good time to ensure that you have prepayment options and that your mortgage can be broken with a penalty if you have to. Believe it or not, some mortgages are not breakable until their maturity date.

Third, challenge yourself to *make payments higher than the minimum*. In fact, it is a good practice to review your mortgage every three months and increase your mortgage payment by $10,

$20 or even $100. Doing this consistently will make dramatic savings on the interest you pay, and in most cases, you'll get used to the extra payment and won't miss the extra money at all! Doing these incremental increases are easier than trying to save for a lump sum payment.

Fourth, pay off credit card debt and car loans first! Work as hard as you can to pay these off quickly, and then use the payment that you were paying for these debts to increase your mortgage payment by the same amount. For example, if your credit card payment was $300 per month, work hard to pay off that debt and then add the $300 payment that you were paying on the credit card to your mortgage payment. This is known as ballooning.

Finally, *review your mortgage every year with your broker*. This is called a *mortgage check-up*. The banks have taught us to "set it and forget it," but leaving our mortgage un-reviewed for more than a year can cost you thousands. Strategies and the products associated with those strategies change every year. It is imperative that you go over any potential savings with your broker. The best news would be that your strategy is doing fine and no changes are needed. Honest brokers will welcome all borrowers into their office for a mortgage check-up, even those who have their mortgage elsewhere. Take advantage of this service.

## Variable or Fixed

This is one of the great debates of most bankers and brokers. In my opinion, it is a distraction from the real issue, which is to save money. Saving money will occur aggressively by paying down your debt above and beyond what the minimum is, regardless of whether the rate is variable or fixed. In the case that you choose a variable rate mortgage, you are flirting with risk when and if rates rise. My suggestion is to increase your mortgage payment *as if* it was a fixed rate at 5% or higher, but let the rate float at the variable. By doing this, you'll be paying thousands off in principle and avoiding interest rate risk when rates do rise. On the contrary, any mortgage rate under 5% is considered historically low, so locking in is not a bad decision; it just costs a bit more than a variable rate to ensure you are not exposed to fluctuations in your payment. Keep in mind that a five-year locked-in mortgage rate will have to come up for renewal in five years, so you will have to face interest rate fluctuations at some point in your mortgage.

### Commissions, Sales Quotas and Points

Earlier, I alluded to the fact that bankers have sales goals and product quotas and that mortgage brokers receive commissions and even points and credits from lenders based on the volume of business sent to those lenders. It is imperative that you have a conversation about those incentives with the banker or broker with whom you are about to potentially do business. Notice how comfortable the broker is while talking about how this system works and how it benefits them. If you have any doubt about how a professional handles this conversation, you may want to move on. An honest and confident broker can talk transparently about how the decision you are going to make affects both you and the broker. It will be harder to have this conversation with a banker because their job will be in jeopardy for disclosing proprietary information.

### The Line of Credit

I once heard my branch manager say that a line of credit is considered an *anchor product* of the bank. This meant that a typical customer who had a line of credit was less likely to leave the bank because the line of credit is not easily switched to another institution. Consequently, lines of credit are harder to qualify for and can ruin your credit rating quicker than a traditional mortgage. Lines of credit are dangerous tools if you don't read the instructions. Here are those instructions:

Lines of credit always float at the prime rate. There are now ways to split them up and fix different parts of your balance, but that complicates your mortgage and almost always results in taking longer to pay it off. It is advisable to use a line of credit with an *all-in-one mortgage,* whereby your banking can be integrated for immediate principle payoff with each dollar going in. If your banker or broker is talking you into converting from a traditional mortgage to a line of credit with a larger credit limit, the chances are that the banker will benefit more than you from the sale. This is assuming that debt freedom is your primary goal for your mortgage debt.

Lines of credit are good tools for investing. I have had several clients us lines of credit to buy one rental property at a time. As they collected the rent, the rent paid off the line of credit. Once the line of credit was at zero, they would use it again to purchase another property. The line of credit is separate from their personal bank account, and the paperwork is organized so that the Canada Revenue Agency can see that the interest is a legitimate write-off with respect to their rental property. I am not saying that this is the best way of investing, but it is an example of how to effectively use a line of credit while minimizing interest rate risk and your ability to pay it back. A line of credit should not to be used to purchase personal items such as cars, ATVs and Plasma screen TVs.

## When To Refinance a Mortgage

Believe it or not, it can be extremely advantageous to break your mortgage contract and refinance. However, knowing when to do it is the hard part. Your banker and broker will love you for breaking your mortgage if you increase it more than $25,000 because that could mean a new commission, but that is not reason enough alone to perform the transaction. Just because your interest rate says 5% and today's rate is at 3.9% does not mean that breaking your mortgage is cost effective. Here's what you need to know in order to justify breaking your current contract.

First, call your lender and ask for the mortgage penalty. GET IT IN WRITING, and record the name of the person to whom you spoke. Lenders can, and have the right, to change the penalty clause at any time without notice. Once you have the penalty information, you can now calculate your potential interest savings. Go to a mortgage calculator that calculates interest costs, such as the one at CMHC.ca (http://www.cmhc.ca/en/co/buho/buho_005.cfm). Include your penalty in the new mortgage balance, but leave your mortgage payment as close to what you are paying now as possible. If the amortization goes down from where you are today or the interest costs between the two comparisons show significant savings, then refinancing is a good thing.

Be careful though. In speaking with many colleagues in the mortgage industry, there are brokers and bankers who will calculate major savings on breaking your mortgage but manipulate the data to come up with those results. Make sure "apples are apples" by comparing the amortizations of your current mortgage to the refinance calculations. For example, if you had 22 years left to pay off your mortgage, ensure that the refinance calculation's amortization is 22 years or less. If it isn't, then you had better look deeper into the calculations!

In the case where you have a considerable amount of debt, such as on credit cards and car loans, add that debt to the penalty costs of breaking and add that to the new mortgage amount (assuming you have enough equity). Now increase your mortgage payment as much as possible to the total of what you were paying before the refinance (mortgage + credit card payment + car loan payment), and if your overall amortization goes down on all debt, then you should do a refinance; it will take you less time to pay off all of your debt by refinancing than by paying it separately as you are right now. Of course, you really should be doing these calculations with your mortgage broker or financial advisor to ensure accuracy and suitability. Everyone's situation is different.

## Product Choice = Confusion

In the chapter *More Choice is More Spending*, we learned that the human brain is not efficient in processing excessive sensory inputs. When subjects were asked to remember a seven-digit number and passed by chocolate cake and fruit salad, the subjects who had to memorize seven digits succumbed to their impulses and chose the chocolate cake. Those who had to remember two digits overwhelmingly chose the fruit salad.

ING Bank knows this human flaw, and this is why they have coined the term *The Un-Mortgage*™. The commercial opens with two neighbours having a conversation while shoveling their driveways during a cold, Canadian Winter. *"Yeah, I just wanted to pay my mortgage off faster."* To which the other neighbour replies, *"Well, if you wanted to pay your mortgage off faster, then just pay your mortgage off faster."* The first neighbour listens with a bewildered look on his face because of the simplicity of the comment. The frame exits to the graphic of all the products and services ING can offer a customer.

As a potential consumer, you think that ING has something unique and powerful that appeals to your goal of becoming debt free. However, all they are offering is a few tips on how you can pre-pay your traditional mortgage when you get it with them. This is done on purpose so that it is difficult for consumers to make a rational choice. Distractions can cause unintended results!

With the confusion about which choice to make, the banks teach their sales forces and their network of mortgage brokers to *sell* you on why their product is unique and the best. They'll list all of the benefits and features, which, by the way, exceed seven items, resulting in a less-than-rational mortgage decision. When I worked in banking, I came across an internal statistic that stated more than 70% of mortgage customers will simply renew their mortgage without a discount. In the world of finances and consumerism, more choice equals more confusion for you and more profit for big business, but it doesn't have to be this way. In fact, debt is simple; what you owe needs to be paid, and the faster you pay it back, the more you save.

There are hundreds of mortgage products on the market, but most are useless regurgitations of existing ones, repackaged to make you think you're receiving something unique. The way to overcome the confusion is to affirm your debt freedom goals and only consider mortgage tools that help you reach your goals. This is best done with both your financial advisor and your mortgage broker.

# MORE TIPS AND RESOURCES
# THAT YOU SHOULD READ!

In the last few chapters, I touched on how you can tackle the two biggest expenses in your life: your home and your mortgage. However, the expenses can't stop there because it will be the small, trivial expenses that eat up your fortune over time. Over the course of my life, I have come across some really amazing, practical and effective books on money. Instead of regurgitating those tips, I will simply list the books here. Make the time to learn more about your finances.

*Rich Dad Poor Dad* by Robert Kiyosaki

*The Four Laws of Debt Free Prosperity* by Blaine Harris and Charles Coonradt

*Secrets of the Millionaire Mind* by T. Harv Ecker

*You're Broke Because You Want to Be* by Larry Winget

*The Richest Man in Babylon* by George S. Clason

Of course, there are thousands of books on money, but these five will give you all the strong foundation you need to dramatically improve your finances.

# MONEY CAN'T MAKE YOU HAPPY BUT IT CAN BE ENJOYED!

We all know the old cliché that money can't buy your happiness, but it can buy you things that you can enjoy! The delusion that we have when we accumulate debt is that we will be happier when we have more stuff.

On the contrary, you will be happier knowing that you did not complicate your life with debt and that when you want to buy something, you can do it with cash. Happy is a life that enjoys the money that has been earned, saved and then spent. Unhappy people are those who continue to bury themselves financially by continually refinancing or making purchases using other people's money.

Money is meant to be spent, so enjoy what you have and save for what you don't!

To your future!

Joe Ornato

# ACKNOWLEDGEMENTS

I'd like to thank my family for teaching me so many things in life and about myself. I appreciate you all: Maggie, Julia, Matteo, Mom, Dad, Jessica, Paulo, Silvio, Rosa and Elvis. It is through others that you discover yourself.

A big thanks goes out to the mortgage industry that taught me so much, and I thank my former staff and colleagues for inspiration, confidence and suggestions.

Thank you to FreisenPress, who helped provide a platform for authors to get their messages out.

Finally, I thank the energy that created us and continues to inspire creativity in living souls.

CPSIA information can be obtained at www.ICGtesting.com
Printed in the USA
LVOW06*1308300813

350063LV00001B/3/P

9 781460 203910